Patrick O'Kane is a Barrister. He is Head of Privacy at a Fortune 500 Company where he helped lead a major GDPR project across a group of more than 100 companies. Previously, he led the Privacy Team at a large group of insurance companies in London. Patrick is the author of the book 'GDPR: Fix it Fast – How to Apply GDPR to your company in ten steps'. He has written on Privacy for numerous journals and magazines.

Patrick is Certified in EU and US Privacy Regulation and was made a Fellow of Information Privacy by the International Association of Privacy Professionals in 2020.

A Practical Guide to GDPR in Financial Services

A Practical Guide to GDPR in Financial Services

Patrick O'Kane

Law Brief Publishing

Published 2021 by Law Brief Publishing, an imprint of Law Brief Publishing Ltd
30 The Parks
Minehead
Somerset
TA24 8BT

www.lawbriefpublishing.com

Paperback: 978-1-913715-83-0

To Katherine

PREFACE

Personal data is vital to any company in financial services. For these companies to survive and prosper, they must process personal data in a way that allows them to:

- Keep up with their competitors
- Understand their customers' wants and needs
- Prevent their customers from using the company to launder money or commit fraud
- Innovate and develop new products
- Reach new prospects

With the financial services becoming more competitive, companies in this sector must be shrewd and agile. They must process data and must do so in innovative ways. They must also be compliant. The EU General Data Protection Regulation ('GDPR') regulates personal data processing. And it carries fines that could pose an existential risk to any company.

This is a practical book that aims to put your company on the right side of GDPR.

The book sets out practical steps including advice on helping your company comply with the rules on:

- Marketing
- Transferring data around the globe
- Sharing data with third parties
- Using Artificial Intelligence
- Processing employee data
- Keeping your data secure, and

- Dealing with customer data access requests

The legal references in this book are correct as of 14 June 2021.

Patrick O'Kane
June 2021

CONTENTS

CHAPTER ONE
GDPR – THE BASICS

This chapter is a refresher on some of the main aspects of GDPR. In this chapter, we look at:

- Financial services
- The key definitions under GDPR
- The Data Protection Principles
- The legal bases for processing personal data

The opening chapter of this book is quite detailed on the legal aspects of GDPR. In the ensuing chapters, I will set out the practical steps financial services firms can take in order to achieve GDPR compliance.

What are financial services?

Financial services are 'professional services involving the investment, lending, and management of money and assets'[1]. There are a wide range of companies in the financial services sector including banks, insurance companies, investment banks, credit card companies, investment managers and accounting firms.

It was estimated that 1.1 million people worked in financial services jobs in the UK in 2020, 3.2% of all jobs. In 2019, the financial services sector contributed £132 billion to the UK economy, 6.9% of total economic output. [2]

---

[1] Oxford English Dictionary – Seventh Edition

[2] House of Commons Library – Financial services: contribution to the UK economy – February 2021

Why is there so much talk about financial services and GDPR?

Financial services companies hold oceans of personal data and given the vast resources and wealth of many financial services firms, they have the means and the technology to process personal data in a myriad of ways. Whilst they do process personal data in more traditional ways, such as for administration, marketing and human resources purposes, they are also known to push the boundaries with personal data. More controversial forms of data processing include activities such as big data analytics, data selling and customer profiling.

There are many more GDPR issues in this sector; financial services companies are often global enterprises and they send data all over the world to their many vendors and suppliers. They also use and pioneer new technology which can have a data protection impact.

GDPR fines against financial services companies have been prevalent and at one point, it was reported that financial services was the sector most frequently fined for GDPR breaches.[3]

GDPR – A refresher

The General Data Protection Regulation (GDPR) is an EU Regulation which regulates the processing of personal data. We discuss the position in the UK immediately below. The GDPR applies to companies processing personal data if those companies are either:

1. In the EU, or
2. Outside the EU but:
    a. offering goods or services to individuals in the EU, or
    b. monitoring the behaviour of those individuals in the EU (for example, by tracking their online behaviour).[4]

[3] The Irish Times – Financial services sector most frequently fined for GDPR breaches. September 19, 2019

[4] GDPR – Article 3

Both Processors and Controllers (see definitions below) are caught by GDPR if they fall into 1. or 2. above.

Does GDPR apply in the UK post-Brexit?

Yes.

GDPR also applies to companies:

1. In the UK, or
2. Outside the UK but:
    a. offering goods or services to individuals in the UK, or
    b. monitoring the behaviour of those individuals in the UK (for example, by tracking their online behaviour).[5]

GDPR became part of the law in all 27 EU member states on 25 May 2018. The UK left the European Union on 31 January 2020. The UK then entered a transition period with the European Union until 31 December 2020. At the end of the transition period, GDPR was incorporated into UK law as the 'UK GDPR' under the European Union (Withdrawal) Act 2018.

The UK Data Protection Act 2018 will continue to supplement and tailor UK GDPR in the UK. UK GDPR largely incorporates EU GDPR save for some clarifications and exceptions.

The ICO has said "*The EU GDPR is an EU Regulation and it no longer applies to the UK. However, if you operate inside the UK, you will need to comply with UK data protection law. The GDPR has been incorporated into UK data protection law as the UK GDPR – so in practice there is little change to the core data protection principles, rights and obligations found in the UK GDPR.... The EU GDPR may also still apply directly to you if you operate in the European Economic Area (EEA), offer goods or services to individuals in the EEA, or monitor the behaviour of individuals in the EEA.*"[6]

[5] Ico.org.uk – UK GDPR

[6] ico.org.uk – Information rights after the end of the transition period – Frequently asked questions

There is a UK GDPR and an EU GDPR. The fundamentals of both of these are the same. Some of the terminology is slightly different within UK GDPR so that it makes sense as a piece of UK legislation.

Where there is no real difference in the rules between UK GDPR and EU GDPR, then this book simply refers to 'GDPR'.

Don't get too hung up on the differences between UK GDPR and EU GDPR. The fundamentals are the same but you should know that there are tweaks here and there that apply to the UK GDPR that are not identical to the law in the EU GDPR. We discuss these further in Chapter 2 – Transfers. This book has a UK focus and primarily refers to GDPR as it relates to the UK. It also refers to other UK law, such as the Data Protection Act 2018.

What is the Data Protection Act 2018?

The Data Protection Act 2018 (DPA 2018) is a UK Law which supplements and amplifies GDPR in the UK in a number of areas.

What is personal data?

The right to access relates to "personal data".

Article 4(1) of GDPR states that 'personal data' means:

- any information
- relating to an identified or identifiable natural person ('data subject').

In other words, personal data is data that is about identifiable human beings.

Sometimes, I use the term 'data' within this book as shorthand for 'personal data'. When the term 'data' is used, it always refers to 'personal data'.

What is an identifiable person?

Personal data is information that relates to an identified or identifiable natural person[7].

You could identify someone from their name or ID number or you could perhaps identify them from something like their phone number or their computer IP address.

Sometimes, we can identify someone directly from the personal data we hold on them. For example, we may have their full name and we therefore don't need any other data to identify the person.

On other occasions, we may not be able to identify the person directly from the data on its own but we may be able to identify the person from the data by linking it to other data or through making further enquiries.

For example, we might have an email in which a customer ID number is mentioned. On its own, the customer number does not reveal anything. However, when enquiries are made, it transpires that the customer number belongs to Neil, a customer of City Bank. The customer number is therefore Neil's personal data. We could not identify Neil directly from the customer number on its own but we could identify him indirectly (e.g. after making further enquiries). Therefore, the customer number is personal data.

What kind of information can be classified as being personal data?

Personal data can come in a variety of forms. Remember, personal data is:

- any information
- relating to an identified or identifiable natural person ('data subject').

Let's take a financial services customer, as an example. Harry owns a van that he uses in his employment as a plumber. He has been insured by

[7] GDPR – Article 4(1)

Motor Insure to drive the van. Motor Insure hold a lot of Harry's personal data including:

A. Harry's name and address.

B. Harry's Date of Birth.

C. Harry's claims history.

D. Harry's previous speeding convictions.

E. Harry's payment history.

F. Harry's bank account details and credit card details.

G. Harry's risk rating as a driver as calculated by Motor Insure.

H. Harry's call recordings from when he phoned to amend his policy.

I. Harry's driving habits as recorded by the telematics equipment (known as a 'black box'), used by Motor Insure to help price Harry's insurance premium.

All of these items at A.- I. are Harry's personal data because they:

- Are data or information, and
- They relate to Harry.

Wide interpretation of personal data

The GDPR definition of personal data is very wide. Virtually any data that relates to an individual (including customers, employees and others) is likely to be their personal data.

What is a data subject?

The human being to whom the personal data relates. Your financial services company is likely to process personal data on a number of different types of data subjects including:

- Customers
- Prospective customers
- Employees
- Job applicants
- Employees from other companies
- Individuals that you track on your website using cookies
- Sole traders who perform services for you
- Visitors to your premises

I often refer to data subjects as 'individuals' throughout the text.

What is a Controller?

A Controller is 'the natural or legal person.....which, alone or jointly with others determines the purposes and means of the processing of personal data'[8].

In other words, they decide how and why the personal data is processed.

The Controller bears the ultimate legal responsibility for processing the personal data. They can be in line for fines if they breach the many rules under GDPR. Your company will be a Controller in respect of much of the personal data they process, including your customer and employee data.

The Controller is the entity that is in the driving seat when it comes to how and why the data is processed.

For example, Harry has been a customer at Motor Insure for 5 years. He holds a Motor Insure Policy for his van. Motor Insure are the Controller in respect of Harry's personal data.

---

[8] GDPR – Article 4(7) GDPR

What are Joint Controllers?

Joint Controllers are 'two or more controllers jointly determining the purposes and means of the processing'. [9]

For example, two insurance companies, Red Insurance and Purple Insurance, have set up a fraud database to help them decide on whether individuals pose a fraud risk. In the database, they add personal data of data subjects who have engaged in fraudulent behaviour. Red and Purple are both in control of the database and it is a joint project. Red and Purple jointly determine the why and how of the personal data processing. This makes them joint controllers.

What is a Processor?

'Processor' means a natural or legal person which processes personal data on behalf of the Controller.[10]

Many companies use third parties to help them carry out their business operations, for example, IT support businesses, couriers, payroll services, waste disposal etc. These companies process personal data on behalf of the Controller.

For example, Diamond Asset Managers use a cloud services provider called Grey Cloud Storage. Diamond process personal data relating to their 3,000 clients. Grey Cloud Storage host all of this data and they sometimes require access to it in order to perform checks and to ensure it is being held securely. Grey do not have any real authority over how the personal data is processed or used and this makes them a Processor.

Before GDPR, Processors had limited legal liability for the data they processed. Post-GDPR, Processors have many more legal obligations than before, including the obligation to:

- Keep personal data secure[11] (See Chapter 9- Security)

---

[9] GDPR – Article 26(1)

[10] GDPR – Article 4(8)

[11] GDPR – Article 32

- Tell the Controller about data breaches (See Chapter 9- Security)[12]
- Get the consent of the Controller if they want to use a Sub-Processor of their own (See Chapter 10 – Dealing with Third Parties)[13]

Processors can be fined under GDPR and they can also be sued by data subjects for GDPR breaches.[14]

Processors must be careful not to step outside the instructions of the Controller. If they do, then this may make the company a Controller, and this brings much more legal liability, in comparison to being a Processor.

Are Controllers, Processors and Joint Controllers always corporations?

In theory, Controllers, Processors and Joint Controllers can be sole traders, such as a self-employed tradesman. A sole trader is a natural person who is the exclusive owner of a business, such as 'Joe's Plumbing Services Limited'. However, in the context of financial services, Controllers, Processors and Joint Controllers are almost always corporations.

Do all companies caught by GDPR have to comply with Data Subject Access Requests?

No. Controllers must comply with Data Subject Access Requests ('DSARs'). Controllers are the companies that bear the ultimate legal responsibility for the data processing under GDPR. Processors have an obligation to help the Controllers with their Access Requests. For

[12] GDPR – Article 33

[13] GDPR – Article 28

[14] GDPR – Article 82

example, Big Bank receive an Access Request from Denise, one of their customers. Some of Denise's data is held by one of Big Bank's processors, a cloud provider company called Grey Cloud. Big Bank ask Grey Cloud to help them find all of Denise's data so they can send it on to her.

See Chapter 13 on GDPR Rights.

What does 'processing' personal data mean?

Processing means *"any operation or set of operations which is performed on personal data"*.[15]

The definition of processing is very wide. Anything that you do with personal data counts as processing it, including *'collection, recording, organisation, structuring, storage, adaptation or alteration, retrieval, consultation, use, disclosure by transmission, dissemination or otherwise making available, alignment or combination, restriction, erasure or destruction'*.

As you can see, doing anything with personal data, including deleting it or storing it, falls under the definition of processing.

What are the special categories of personal data?

There are certain categories of personal data that require extra protection under GDPR Article 9. These categories of personal data are known as the special categories of personal data. They are sometimes referred to as 'sensitive personal data'.

The special categories are:[16]

- personal data revealing **racial or ethnic origin**
- personal data revealing **political opinions**

---

[15] GDPR – Article 4(2)

[16] GDPR – Article 9(1)

- personal data revealing **religious or philosophical beliefs**
- personal data revealing **trade union membership**
- **genetic data**
- **biometric data** (where used for identification purposes)
- data concerning **health**
- data concerning a person's **sex life** and
- data concerning a person's **sexual orientation**

Do financial services firms hold special category personal data?

Financial services firms often hold special category personal data for a number of purposes. For example, insurance companies often collect personal data relating to the health of their customers in order to be able to help them price their policies. As another example, financial services firms may also collect personal data relating to the race and ethnic origin of their employees, for equality monitoring purposes.

The Data Protection Principles

There are a set of principles within GDPR that set out how personal data must be processed. These principles are the most important part of GDPR.

As professionals within financial services, we are often asked by colleagues about 'whether GDPR allows us' to carry out a certain activity.

In deciding whether a particular activity is permitted under GDPR, you should first look at the principles and ask yourself whether the activity is consistent with these principles.

The principles are set out at Article 5 of GDPR.[17] They may not have all the answers about the nuances of your particular problem, but they should be your first port of call.

The table below sets out each principle. Although there are many things that a company must consider in terms of staying in compliance with each principle, the table below gives one brief example of how each principle may impact a financial services firm.

Key Principle:	**What the rule says in GDPR:**	**One example of how the principle may impact financial services firms:**
1.Lawfulness, fairness and transparency	Personal data shall be processed lawfully, fairly and in a transparent manner in relation to the data subject.	Financial services firms must be open with their customers about how their personal data is used in their Website Privacy Notices.
2.Purpose limitation	Personal data shall be collected for specified, explicit and legitimate purposes and not further processed in a manner that is incompatible with those purposes.	Firms cannot collect customer data for one purpose and then go behind the customer's back to use it for an entirely different purpose.
3.Data minimisation	Personal data shall be adequate, relevant and limited to what is necessary in relation to the purposes for which it is processed.	Firms cannot use more data than is necessary for a particular purpose. For example, if an Asset Manager has too many boxes on an application form that collects more personal data than is needed, they are in breach of this principle.

[17] GDPR – Article 5(1)-(2)

4.Accuracy	Personal data shall be accurate and, where necessary, kept up to date.	Firms should take reasonable steps to ensure the data they retain on customers is accurate and they should allow customers to update it.
5.Storage limitation	Personal data shall be kept in a form which permits identification of data subjects for no longer than is necessary for the purposes for which the personal data is processed.	Customer and employee records should not be kept for longer than is necessary for the purposes for which the data was collected. For example, if an employee left the firm a decade ago and their data is no longer needed, then the data should be deleted. Firms should draw up Data Retention Schedules to set out how long personal data is to be retained.
6.Security	Personal data shall be processed in a manner that ensures appropriate security of the personal data, including protection against unauthorised or unlawful processing and against accidental loss, destruction or damage, using appropriate technical or organisational measures.	Firms should ensure they have appropriate security including: a. Technology like anti-virus, anti-malware and Data Loss Prevention Software, and b. Organisational measures such as training staff on data protection. This ensures personal data is not lost or compromised.

7.**Accountability**	The Controller shall be responsible for, and be able to demonstrate compliance with the above principles.	Firms should keep records of the way in which they process personal data in compliance with GDPR, in case a Regulator ever asks for evidence of their data processing. Firms must be compliant with GDPR, but must also be able to "demonstrate" that compliance.

It is a potentially serious matter for a firm to breach any of the data protection principles.

If a financial services firm breaches any of the principles, as set out in Article 5 of GDPR, then they can be liable for the higher level of fines under GDPR (4% of Global Annual Turnover and 20 million). [18]

A firm can also be sued by a data subject such as a customer or an individual if they 'suffer any material or non-material damage' as a result of any infringement of GDPR, including the Article 5 principles.[19]

Always keep the principles in mind when you are building your Data Protection Program within your company.

The legal bases for processing personal data

When your firm processes personal data relating to a particular individual, it must have a legal basis (sometimes called 'the lawfulness conditions') in place that allows them to carry out each aspect of the personal data processing.

To draw an analogy, each aspect of personal data processing conducted by your firm is like crossing a river. The legal bases are bridges. They give

[18] GDPR – Article 83(5)(a)

[19] GDPR – Article 82(1)

you the support you need to cross the river. You cannot cross the river safely unless a bridge is in place.

For example, if a bank wishes to send a marketing email to a customer, it must have a legal basis in place to allow them to do that. Equally, if an insurance company wants to process data relating to a customer's speeding convictions to help them to determine how to price a customer's policy, then they need a legal basis in place to permit them to do this.

In other words, any time you use personal data, you need a legal basis to do so.

The legal bases for processing appear at Article 6 of GDPR and they are set out below:

a) **Consent of the data subject** – The data subject has given consent to the processing of his or her personal data for one or more specific purposes.[20]

b) **Contractual necessity** – Processing is necessary for the performance of a contract to which the data subject is party or in order to take steps, at the request of the data subject, prior to entering into a contract.[21]

c) **Legal obligation** – Processing is necessary for compliance with a legal obligation to which the Controller is subject.[22]

d) **Vital interests of an individual** – Processing is necessary in order to protect the vital interests of the data subject or of another natural person.[23]

e) **Performance of a task in the public interest** – Processing is necessary for the performance of a task carried out in the public

[20] GDPR – Article 6(1)(a)

[21] GDPR – Article 6(1)(b)

[22] GDPR – Article 6(1)(c)

[23] GDPR – Article 6(1)(d)

interest or in the exercise of official authority vested in the Controller.[24]

f) **Legitimate interest of your firm** – Processing is necessary for the purposes of the legitimate interests pursued by the Controller or by a third party, except where such interests are overridden by the interests or fundamental rights and freedoms of the data subject.[25]

There is no one legal basis that works better than the other available legal bases but it is up to you to judge which legal basis is most appropriate in the circumstances based on the type of data processing you are doing and on your relationship with the data subject. Be careful about choosing your lawful basis; if it is not a valid or logical legal basis then you may potentially be breaching GDPR by processing the personal data.

a), b) c) and f) are likely to be the most commonly used legal bases for personal data processing in relation to financial services and we are going to look at each in turn in the context of financial services.

The 4 legal bases most commonly used in financial services

1. Consent

Obtaining consent is an important legal basis that can permit financial services firms to process personal data. However, it is incorrect to suggest that firms always need consent in order to process personal data.

Under Article 4(11) of GDPR, consent is

"Any freely given, specific, informed and unambiguous indication of the data subject's wishes by which he or she, by a statement or by a clear affirmative action, signifies agreement to the processing of personal data relating to him or her".

In other words, consent must be:

---

[24] GDPR – Article 6(1)(e)

[25] GDPR – Article 6(1)(f)

- **Free** – You cannot twist the data subject's arm to get their consent by telling them that they must provide consent to you and telling them that you will not provide your services if they do not consent.[26]
- **Specific and unbundled** – The individual must be consenting to something specific and unbundled. For example, asking the individual to consent to a lengthy page of terms and conditions would not work because this consent would not be specific enough.
- **Informed** – Individuals must know what they are consenting too. You should provide information at or near the consent box to allow them to understand what their consent means.
- **Opt in** – Consent must be by clear affirmative action. You cannot pre-tick a box for an individual as this would not be valid consent. You must let the individual tick the box if they are happy to give you the consent.

Individuals have the right to withdraw their consents at any time. [27]

Consent will not always be an appropriate legal basis to process personal data under GDPR. For example, if a financial institution wants to send personal data relating to a customer to law enforcement because it believes that fraud may have occurred, then it will not and should not seek the consent of the customer to do so. It would be better to rely on one of the alternative legal bases under GDPR such as Legal Obligation or Legitimate Interest.

Similarly, obtaining valid consent from your employees may also be difficult. Consents must be free. There is always an imbalance in the employer-employee relationship because the employer is usually the one with much of the power in the relationship. As a result, employees may feel obliged to give their consent to their employer when they ask for it.

---

[26] GDPR – Article 7(4)

[27] GDPR – Article 7(3)

2. Contractual necessity

Often, you will process personal data under GDPR because the processing is necessary for the performance of a contract to which the **data subject is party.**[28]

The ICO says "*You can rely on this lawful basis if you need to process someone's personal data:*

to deliver a contractual service to them; or

because they have asked you to do something before entering into a contract (eg provide a quote)."[29]

For example, Sally is seeking a quote from Mega Insurance. Mega needs to process Sally's name, address and date of birth to be able to provide her with the insurance quote. Mega can rely on contractual necessity to process Sally's data in this instance.

Remember, if you seek to rely on this as a basis for a particular aspect of personal data processing, then it must be a "necessity" for the performance of the contract. In other words, you cannot rely on it as a matter of convenience. It must be necessary for the performance of the contract for you to process the personal data in this particular way.

3. Legal obligation

Under this legal basis, a Controller can process personal data if the processing is necessary for compliance with a legal obligation to which the Controller is subject.[30]

For example, a financial institution may wish to process a customer's personal data for the purposes of anti-money laundering ('AML') checks, before allowing a customer to open an account. The financial institution may be entitled to process the personal data for AML checks if the

[28] GDPR – Article 6(1)(b)

[29] ICO Guidance – Guide to the GDPR

[30] GDPR – Article 6(1)(c)

processing is necessary in order to comply with a legal obligation under anti-money laundering legislation.

There must be a legal obligation in place which obliges the financial institution to act in this way. If you are seeking to rely on a legal obligation in order to process personal data, then check carefully to ensure it is a legal obligation or duty.

4. Necessary for the legitimate interest of your firm

Again, processing under this ground is quite commonplace in financial services companies.

A firm is permitted to process an individual's data under this ground if the processing is:

- *"Necessary for the purposes of the legitimate interests pursued by the controller or by a third party, except where such interests are overridden by the interests or fundamental rights and freedoms of the data subject".*[31]

This is often thought of as one of the most controversial legal bases on which to rely.

What does the legitimate interests of your firm mean? A reasonable interpretation of this can mean that the personal data may be processed for a legitimate business purpose by your firm.

For example, an Asset Management company may be able to rely on legitimate interests to disclose their employee data to an outsourced payroll provider to help the Asset Management company calculate the wages that are due to each employee.

If you wish to rely on this ground, then you must ensure that you are being fair to the individual involved. One must make sure that the legitimate interest that you seek to assert is not overridden by the interests or fundamental rights and freedoms of the data subject. In other words,

[31] GDPR – Article 6(1)(f)

if the type of data processing is not within the reasonable expectation of the individual, then it would be difficult to rely on this ground.[32]

What happens when firms process special category personal data?

It is more complex to process special category personal data.

If your firm is processing special category data, such as personal data relating to race, politics, religion, genetics, biometrics, health, sex life or sexuality, then you will need one of the Article 6 legal bases we have set out above (see para above 'The Legal bases for processing personal data'). **You will also need a further legal basis under Article 9 of GDPR.**

This table sets out the further legal basis under Article 9 that you will need in order to process personal data.

Legal basis under GDPR Article 9 to allow you to process special category personal data:	More detail:
(a) Explicit consent	The data subject has given explicit consent to the processing of the personal data.
(b)Employment, social security and social protection law[33]	Processing is necessary for the purposes of carrying out the obligations in the field of employment and social security and social protection law.

[32] GDPR – Recital 47

[33] If you are relying on conditions (b) (Employment law obligation), (h) (Health or social care), (i) Public health or (j) (Archiving, research and statistics), you also need to meet an additional condition in UK law, set out in Part 1 of Schedule 1 of the DPA 2018. (h) (i) and (j) rarely come up in financial services so it is unlikely this will impact your firm.

(c) Vital interests	Processing is necessary to protect the vital interests of the data subject or of another natural person where the data subject is physically or legally incapable of giving consent.
(d) Not-for-profit bodies	Processing is carried out in the course of its legitimate activities with appropriate safeguards by a foundation, association or any other not-for-profit body.
(e) Made public by the data subject	Processing relates to personal data which is manifestly made public by the data subject.
(f) Legal claims and judicial acts	Processing is necessary for the establishment, exercise or defence of legal claims.
(g) Substantial public interest conditions[34]	Processing is necessary for reasons of substantial public interest **If you are relying on this condition, then you will need a further legal basis under the Data Protection Act 2018 (see below).**
(h) Health or social care	Processing is necessary for the purposes of the provision of health or social care.
(i) Public health	Processing is necessary for reasons of public interest in the area of public health.
(j) Archiving, research and statistics	Processing is necessary for archiving purposes in the public interest or for scientific or historical research.

[34] To rely on the substantial public interest condition in the UK, you must also comply with a condition under Part 2 of Schedule 1 of the DPA 2018.

Substantial public interest – Relying on this in the context of financial services in order to process special category personal data

If your company is:

- Processing special category data, such as data on race etc, **and**
- It is seeking to rely on the legal ground of 'substantial public interest' under Article 9 of GDPR to allow them to process that personal data, then it will also need to:
- Meet one of 23 specific substantial public interest conditions, set out in Part 2 of Schedule 1 of the DPA 2018.

I'm confused! My company wants to process special category data and it wants to rely on 'substantial public interest' under Article 9 of GDPR to do that. What else do I need to know?

As we said above, if you are relying on 'substantial public interest' to process special category personal data, then you also need to meet one of 23 specific substantial public interest conditions set out in Schedule 1 of the Data Protection Act 2018.

These are the conditions that may permit you to process special category personal data on the grounds of substantial public interest.

Some of these conditions are very useful in a financial services context.

The conditions of substantial public interest include processing that is necessary for:

- Preventing fraud[35]
- Suspicion of terrorist financing or money laundering[36]
- Insurance[37]

---

[35] Data Protection Act 2018 Schedule 1, Part 2, para 14

[36] Data Protection Act 2018 Schedule 1, Part 2, para 15

[37] Data Protection Act 2018 Schedule 1, Part 2, para 20

- Occupational pensions[38]

It is up to you to decide which of the conditions best apply to you and to make a judgment on whether they allow you to process the special category personal data.

For example:

- Peter Smith has an insurance policy with Big Insure which covers him in the event that his health deteriorates, and he is no longer able to work.
- Peter made a claim on the policy last month.
- Big Insure believe Peter's claim is fraudulent.
- Big Insure decide to pass information on Peter to their external claims investigator so they can investigate Peter's claim.
- Big Insure need a lawful basis under GDPR Article 6 and GDPR Article 9 to send Peter's health personal data to their claims investigator.
- They rely on:
    - "legitimate interests" under Article 6 of GDPR.
    - "substantial public interest" under Article 9 of GDPR.
- Because they are relying on substantial public interest under Article 9, they need a further condition under Part 2 of Schedule 1 of the DPA 2018 Data Protection Act 2018. In this case, they rely on "preventing fraud".
- Big Insure send Peter's data to the claims investigator.

[38] Data Protection Act 2018 Schedule 1, Part 2, para 21

Appropriate policy document

To rely on the substantial public interest conditions (ie when you want to process special category data by relying on the substantial public interest condition), you also need an appropriate, written policy in place in your company. This is to ensure you behave in a compliant way when you are processing the personal data whilst relying on the substantial public interest conditions:

The ICO says:

"An appropriate policy document is a short document outlining your compliance measures and retention policies for special category data. The DPA 2018 says you must have one in place for almost all of the substantial public interest conditions (and also for the employment, social security and social protection condition), as a specific accountability and documentation measure."[39]

Summary of relying on the law on Legal Bases for special category data

To reiterate, in order to process special category personal data, your firm will need:

- One of the legal bases under Article 6 of GDPR as set out above under the section entitled '**The Legal Bases for processing personal data**' (which include consent, contractual necessity, legal obligation of the Controller, vital interests, public interest and legitimate interests), and
- A further legal basis as set out under Article 9 of GDPR and in the table immediately above

For example:

- Big Bank have to process special category data relating to Dave.

[39] Ico.org.uk – What are the substantial public interest conditions?

- Dave is one of their employees.
- Dave has issued a legal claim against Big Bank.
- He alleges that Big Bank have given him so much work that it has caused him to suffer from stress and anxiety.
- Big Bank are preparing their defence to the claim and they wish to send their lawyers some of the details they hold relating to Dave's mental health.
- Big Bank need a legal basis under Article 6 of GDPR and Article 9 of GDPR to share the personal data with their lawyers.

In other words, Big Bank need two grounds, one under Article 6, and one under Article 9 of GDPR. They can rely on:

- Article 6 – Necessary for the purposes of Big Bank's legitimate interest, and
- Article 9 – Necessary in order to defend a legal claim

Big Bank are able to send the personal data to their lawyers.

Criminal Offence Data

There are rules in place around processing of personal data relating to criminal convictions and offences and alleged offences [40]('criminal data').

For example, if a bank or insurance company carries out checks on whether a person has criminal convictions as part of their fraud or AML checks, then they are processing criminal personal data.

As with special category data, it is legally complex to process criminal data so you should first ask yourself whether you can achieve the same goal without processing the criminal data.

[40] Data Protection Act 2018 – Section 10

Firstly, you must still have a lawful basis for your processing under Article 6. (See 'The legal bases for processing personal data under Article 6' above).

Secondly, you must also have an appropriate Data Protection Act 2018 Schedule 1 condition to process the criminal data.

The Schedule 1 conditions that might be most appropriate in financial services for processing criminal data are:

- Preventing or detecting unlawful acts[41]
- Protecting the public against dishonesty[42]
- Preventing fraud[43]
- Suspicion of terrorist financing or money laundering[44]
- Consent[45]
- Legal claims[46]
- Insurance[47]

Check these conditions within the UK Data Protection Act 2018.

To make matters even more complex, there are different rules across other EU states which only allow the processing of criminal data in very specific circumstances, so if you are doing it across the EU, then you need to check that you are compliant in each member state.

---

[41] Data Protection Act 2018 – Schedule 1, Part 2, Para 10

[42] Data Protection Act 2018 – Schedule 1, Part 2, Para 11

[43] Data Protection Act 2018 – Schedule 1, Part 2, Para 14

[44] Data Protection Act 2018 – Schedule 1, Part 2, Para 15

[45] Data Protection Act 2018 – Schedule 1, Part 3, Para 29

[46] Data Protection Act 2018 – Schedule 1, Part 3, Para 33

[47] Data Protection Act 2018 – Schedule 1, Part 2, Para 20

The potential consequences of failing to comply with GDPR

- **A Fine** – Breach of GDPR can lead to a fine. The maximum fine under GDPR is up to 20 million EUR or 4% of the total worldwide annual turnover, whichever is higher. The maximum fines can be levied against firms for breaches of the rules relating to the Data Protection Principles and the Legal Bases as set out earlier in this chapter. Fines levied by Regulators must be 'proportionate'[48].

- **A ban** – The Data Protection supervisory authorities in the EU and the UK have corrective powers and can ban firms from carrying out personal data processing. [49]

- **Legal action** – Any person who suffers damage as a result of a breach of any of their GDPR rights can sue the Controller or Processor for compensation [50].

- **Reputational Damage** – Firms may suffer reputational damage if they receive a fine or some form of regulatory sanction which can be damaging and expensive.

[48] GDPR – Article 83(5)

[49] GDPR – Article 58(2)(f)

[50] GDPR – Article 82(1)

CHAPTER TWO

INTERNATIONAL DATA TRANSFERS IN FINANCIAL SERVICES

Introduction

If personal data is to be transferred to another country, then GDPR demands that sufficient protections are in place for that personal data. These Transfer Rules are set out in GDPR. [51]The rules apply to all data transfers regardless of the amount of personal data being transferred, for example, whether it is one person's data or the data of 1,000 people.

Why do companies transfer personal data around the globe?

Global companies need to transfer personal data to countries around the globe for a multiplicity of reasons. For example, a financial services company may send personal data to a different country for:

- **Staff administration** e.g. sending employee data to Group HR in another country
- **Storage** e.g. sending customer data to a cloud provider in another country
- **Operations** e.g. sending customer personal data to a marketing company

Personal data – Sending personal data to third parties in different countries

Companies transfer data to all sorts of third parties abroad including:

- Companies within your group

[51] GDPR – Chapter V

- Suppliers such as cloud providers, IT service providers or payroll providers
- Corporate clients

What does this chapter focus on?

As this is a UK textbook, we want to look at the rules on sending personal data outside the UK under UK GDPR.

We will look at those rules and how they impact your company.

We also deal briefly with data transfers from the EU (if your company has a presence in the EU).

What is a data transfer?

A data transfer is a transfer of personal information outside the country.

Here are some examples of personal data transfers:

1. An insurance company in the UK emails a list of its employees in the Marketing team to company HQ in the US.
2. An Asset Management Company uploads profiles of its company directors in the UK to its global website and these profiles are viewable across the globe.
3. An accounting firm in the EU decides to store all of its client database information in the cloud. The cloud services provider stores the data in Singapore.
4. A stockbroker in London emails details of personal data relating to one client to its office in Tokyo.
5. A bank in France is acquired by a company in the US. As a result, the HR department is moved from Paris to Dallas.

Is putting personal data on a website a transfer?

Yes. The ICO says that "*the restricted transfer takes place when someone outside the UK accesses the personal data via the website*".[52]

Do you need to transfer at all?

Firstly, ask yourself whether the transfer of data needs to be done at all. A company should not transfer personal data if the same goal can be achieved without transferring the personal data at all such as by fully anonymising the personal data.

What are the rules in the UK?

If you are caught by UK GDPR, then you must understand the rules in place relating to sending personal data outside the UK.

Who does UK GDPR apply to?

The UK GDPR applies to processing carried out by organisations operating within the UK. It also applies to organisations outside the UK that offer goods or services to individuals in the UK.[53]

UK GDPR – I am confused! Is this different from EU GDPR?

The ICO has said "*These UK transfer rules broadly mirror the EU GDPR rules, but the UK has the independence to keep the framework under review.*"[54]

---

[52] ICO Guide to GDPR – Page 254

[53] ICO Guide to GDPR – Page 8

[54] ICO Guide to GDPR – Page 250

Our company is caught by GDPR. What must we do in order to be allowed to send personal data from the UK to another country?

In order for the transfer to be allowed, it must fall into one of the following three categories[55]:

1. **Safe country** – It is going to a safe country i.e. a country that the UK Government considers safe, OR
2. **Appropriate safeguard** – There is an appropriate safeguard in place e.g. although the data is being sent to a country that is **not** on the UK's list of safe countries, there is a contract between the sending and receiving companies covering data protection, OR
3. **Exception** – There is an exception in place e.g. the company has the consent of the data subject to send the personal data outside the UK.

We look at these three points in more detail below.

1. Safe countries

As of May 2021, the UK Government has decided there is no restriction on a UK company sending personal data to a company in the EEA (although this will be kept under review). The EEA includes EU countries and also Iceland, Liechtenstein and Norway.

There are some further countries to which you can send personal data unrestricted. These are known as the 'safe countries'. This means your company can send personal data from the UK to a company in any of these countries freely.

The safe countries[56] are:

- Counties in the EEA
- Gibraltar
- Andorra
- Argentina

[55] GDPR – Articles 45-49

[56] ICO Guide to GDPR – Page 255

- Guernsey
- Isle of Man
- Israel
- Jersey
- New Zealand
- Switzerland
- Uruguay
- Japan – If the receiving entity is in the private sector.
- Canada – This only covers data that is subject to Canada's Personal Information Protection and Electronic Documents Act (PIPEDA).

2. Appropriate safeguards

If you want to send personal data from the UK to a country that is not on the list of safe countries above, then you need something called an "appropriate safeguard" [57] in place. For example, Silver Bank is based in the UK. They have a customer database that they want to send to one of their group companies in Australia. They need to make sure there is a mechanism in place that will allow them to carry out this transfer from the UK to Australia.

There are a number of appropriate safeguards under GDPR. However, the two main mechanisms that are probably the most relevant to companies in financial services are:

a. **Standard Contractual Clauses** (**'SCCs'**) – Standard Contractual Clauses[58] (sometimes referred to as 'model clauses') are the most commonly used and perhaps the best solution for financial services companies wishing to send personal data to a third country. They are recognised by UK GDPR.

   SCCs are basically a set of clauses that you ask the receiving company to sign. In signing them, the receiving company agrees

[57] GDPR – Article 46

[58] GDPR – Article 46(2)(c)

to provide an adequate level of data protection for the data they receive.

There are different types of SCCs including SCCs for Controller to Controller transfers and SCCs for Controller to Processor transfers.

The European Commission published new SCCs in June 2021. The new SCCs were updated to make sure they were aligned with the European Court of Justice Schrems II decision (see below) and GDPR. Companies subject to EU GDPR should transition over to these new SCCs within 18 months. New SCCs for companies subject to UK GDPR are expected soon.

b. **Binding Corporate Rules** – Binding Corporate Rules [59]('BCRs') allow the transfer of data within a group of companies. They are a set of rules that global companies can sign up to. It is like a company charter that your company signs up to, setting out how it will keep data safe when it is transferred abroad. Companies apply to the UK Regulator, the ICO, to put BCRs in place. It can take up to 2 years for the approval process to go through.

BCRs can be a good solution for global financial services companies. It means that your company has one master document that can legitimize the data transfers between the different companies within the group. This means that you do not have to draft hundreds or even thousands of contracts with the Standard Contractual Clauses (see 1. Above) for all the many transfers that you do within your group. This can be more cost-efficient over the longer term as it avoids the expense of drafting hundreds of contracts a year.

3. **Exceptions**

[59] GDPR – Article 47

There are a number of exceptions [60]to the rules set out above in relation to the transfer of personal data. These are set out below.

1. **Consent** – Has the individual given his or her explicit consent to the restricted transfer?
2. **Contract** – Do you have a contract with the individual? Is the restricted transfer necessary for

   you to perform that contract?
3. **Contract benefits another** – Do you have (or are you entering into) a contract with an individual which benefits another individual whose data is being transferred?
4. **Public interest** – You need to make the restricted transfer for important reasons of public interest.
5. **Protecting the vital interests of someone** – You need to make the restricted transfer to protect the vital interests of an individual. He or she must be physically or legally incapable of giving consent.
6. **Public register** – You are making the restricted transfer from a public register.
7. **A one-off** – You are making a one-off restricted transfer and it is in your compelling legitimate interests.[61]

The exceptions are narrowly interpreted and are difficult to rely on for that reason. If an exception applies, then you do not need to transfer the data to a safe country nor do you need an appropriate safeguard to make the transfer (see above). The ICO has said you should only use them as exceptions and that as a "general rule" you should rely on safe countries or appropriate safeguards to make transfers.[62]

[60] GDPR – Article 49

[61] ICO Guide to GDPR – Page 261-265

[62] ICO Guide to GDPR – Page 261-265

What if my company is also subject to EU GDPR?

Your financial services company may be subject to EU and UK GDPR. The UK and EU GDPR rules are largely the same.

Your company may be subject to EU GDPR if it is:

1. In the EU, or is

2. Established outside the EU but is offering goods/services (paid or for free) or is monitoring the behaviour of individuals in the EU.[63] [64]

If your company is caught by EU GDPR, then it must:

- **Safe countries** – Send the data to one of the EU Commission's designated safe countries (Andorra, Argentina, Canada (commercial organisations), Faroe Islands, Guernsey, Israel, Isle of Man, Japan, Jersey, New Zealand, Switzerland, Uruguay.)[65] As of June 2021, the UK is also a safe country and data can be transferred from the EU and wider European Economic Area (EEA) to the UK. **OR**
- **Have an appropriate safeguard in place** – Such as standard contractual clauses or BCRs, **OR**
- **Be able to rely on an exception** – Such as consent or public interest. (See para above 'Exceptions'.)

Schrems II – Your 3-minute guide

The European Court of Justice (CJEU) gave judgment in a case called Schrems II in July 2020.

Cases from the Court of Justice of the European Union form part of EU law. The case of Schrems II is also part of retained UK case law, as it was

---

[63] The European Commission – Who does the data protection law apply to? https://ec.europa.eu

[64] GDPR – Article 3

[65] Ec.europa.eu – Adequacy Decisions

decided before the UK left the European Union so the case continues to apply in the UK post-Brexit.

There was a framework called Privacy Shield that allowed companies to transfer personal data from the EU to the United States.

The CJEU decided that Privacy Shield was no longer valid.

They also said that Standard Contractual Clauses were valid but they added some caveats to this.

The bottom line is that companies (whether they are in the UK or EU) can still use Standard Contractual Clauses to transfer personal data to a third country.

The CJEU said that when companies send personal data to a third country under Standard Contractual Clauses, then they must be satisfied that the country to which the data is sent has a level of protection for the personal data that is "*essentially equivalent*" to that in the European Union or UK.

If the protection is not essentially the equivalent (for example, because the third country's government might snoop or access the personal data), then the companies must put "*supplementary measures*" in place to help protect the data.

These supplementary measures can be:

- Contractual – e.g. clauses that ensure the data is protected.
- Technical – e.g. making sure encryption is used.
- Organisational – e.g. making sure staff are trained so that the data being sent is protected.

The ICO has said that you must undertake a risk assessment to be satisfied that the data subjects of the data that is being sent to the third country will have a level of protection that is essentially the equivalent to that under the UK or EU data protection regime. [66]

[66] ICO Guide to GDPR – Page 256

Legal basis to transfer

Even if you have a valid transfer mechanism in place such as SCCs, remember that you also need a legal basis to transfer the personal data. The legal bases are set out under Article 6 of GDPR, (as well as Article 9 if the personal data is special category personal data) and they include consent, contractual necessity or legitimate interests. See Chapter 1 for more details.

Practical steps

1. **Map your data flows** – Try to understand where your data is being sent in the world as I have set out above.
2. **Contracts** – Ascertain which data transfers are not covered by standard contractual clauses and work to ensure these clauses are put in place to cover the transfers. Start with your higher risk transfers, such as transfers involving large amounts of data to cloud providers or processors. Work with your Group Legal Function to ensure these contractual clauses are rolled out.
3. **Risk Assessment** – As explained above in relation to the Schrems II case, companies must now do a risk assessment when sending data to a third country. They must do this to be satisfied that the data that is being sent to the third country with a data protection regime that has a level of protection that is essentially equivalent to that under the UK or EU data protection regime. Try to put a risk assessment regime in place to deal with this.
4. **BCRs** – Work out whether your company would benefit from having binding corporate rules in place to govern its transfers within the Group. This may be more efficient than drafting up contracts to cover all the different transfers that you do.
5. **Policy** – Make sure you include a section setting out your company rules on Data Transfers, in your Data Protection Policy. Ensure staff are trained on their obligations on transferring data in your Staff Privacy Training.

CHAPTER THREE

RISK ASSESSING NEW PROJECTS AND PRODUCTS UNDER GDPR

What are DPIAs?

A Data Protection Impact Assessment (DPIA) is a risk assessment tool to mitigate risk in relation to personal data processing.

The Data Protection Impact Assessment is usually a form (such as a webform). The form is completed by the person in charge of the project. The person in charge explains what the project is and how personal data is used.

The DPIA form is then assessed by the company Data Protection Officer (DPO) or compliance expert if you do not have a DPO. The DPO then either:

- Approves the DPIA if they believe the project can go ahead, or
- Rejects the DPIA if they believe the project is too risky.

DPIAs – What is the point?

DPIAs can help your company avoid trouble later on down the road. It helps you put controls in place to mitigate risk on your projects. This can help you avoid fines and data breaches later on.

DPIAs – Do they have to be a bore?

No. Your company can put a slick and efficient process in place to try to mitigate the risks of your personal data processing. You do not want to drown your business in red tape. It helps to have a process in place that is simple for your employees to understand so they can complete and process the form efficiently.

At what stage in the project should you do the DPIA?

The DPIA should be done at the start of each new project so that the risks can be mitigated before the new project is rolled out. Otherwise your company may spend time and money on a project that must be stopped at a later stage because it is not compliant with GDPR.

3 tips on making the DPIA process more efficient

1. **Simple form** – Try and put a simple DPIA form in place that the employees in your company will understand and be able to complete.
2. **Don't be afraid to reject a DPIA** – If you are the Data Protection Officer, then do not be afraid to reject a DPIA form if you believe that the company should not be processing data in the way that is proposed on the DPIA. Breaching GDPR can carry big fines so make sure any project you approve is consistent with GDPR and other data protection laws and regulations.
3. **Pick up the phone** – If you are responsible for approving DPIAs, you may not fully understand the project from the form that has been submitted. Pick up the phone to the form submitter and talk through the project with them before coming to a decision on whether to accept or reject the form.

Making DPIAs stick

Tell your staff about the DPIA process in company communications and staff training.

It is advisable to set out the rules on completing DPIAs in your staff Data Protection Policy. If staff proceed to bring new projects to market that involve personal data and if they have not followed the company's Data Protection Policy, then they will have breached the policy and should be disciplined.

What kinds of risk mitigations can you put in place?

There are many different types of risk mitigation. 5 brief examples of potential risk mitigation are set out below:

- **Using less personal data** – Perhaps the aim of the project can be reached by using less data or through anonymising the personal data.

- **Putting better security controls in place** – You may be able to improve the data security on the project by using better technical measures such as:
    - Encryption
    - Pseudonymisation (e.g. removing customer names from a database and giving each person a number and keeping the names separately)
    - Anti-malware
- **Training staff** – You may be able to reduce the risks by training staff to ensure they don't lose or misuse personal data that is entrusted to them in the project.

- **Telling Data Subjects** – Do you need to tell any data subjects about what you are doing in the project by updating your privacy notices? (See Chapter12 for more rules on Privacy Notices. Do you need to seek their consent?

- **Disclosing data to third parties** – If the project involves sharing personal data with third parties, then contracts should be in place so the third party does not misbehave when handling data you have entrusted to them. See **Chapter 10 on Contracts.**

Who submits the DPIA form within a company?

There is no hard and fast rule. DPIAs are usually submitted by the person in charge of the project or someone equally knowledgeable about the project.

For example, if the Marketing Department are seeking approval for a new tool that records details on prospective customers, then the person within Marketing who is seeking to roll out the new tool should submit the DPIA form.

Have there been any fines for failing to comply with the rules on DPIAs?

Yes. In one example, the Swedish Data Protection Supervisory Authority (the 'Datainspektionen') fined an education board £17,000[67] for breaches of GDPR including failing to conduct a DPIA before rolling out a Facial Recognition Technology trial within one of its schools.

In theory, breach of the DPIA rules can attract fines of up to 10m and 2% of global annual turnover,[68]so it pays to have a good process in place.

When is a DPIA legally required under GDPR?

There are some cases in which a DPIA is legally required under GDPR.

1. **High Risk** – We must carry out a DPIA where data processing is likely to result in 'a high risk to the rights and freedoms of natural persons'.[69]
2. **Profiling/Special Category Data/Monitoring**- We must also carry out a DPIA if there is:
    - Profiling e.g. building profiles of your customers.
    - Large scale special category processing e.g. processing large amounts of health data.
    - Large scale monitoring e.g. monitoring people by online tracking or CCTV.[70]

---

67 https://www.bbc.co.uk/news/technology-49489154.

68 GDPR – Article 83(4)(a)

69 GDPR – Article 35(1)

70 GDPR – Article 35(3)

What if a DPIA is NOT Legally required?

Some companies wish to conduct DPIAs for all new forms of data processing regardless of whether they fall under 1 or 2 in the paragraph above.

If you wish to roll out DPIAs more widely within your company, then you might consider making DPIAs mandatory for all new projects that process personal data. You can do a shorter DPIA form for less risky projects, such as those which do not process a lot of personal data.

Are DPIAs only for new projects or should we also do them for existing projects?

Any high-risk processing mandates a DPIA whether this is a new project or something your company has been doing for a long time. [71]

It is advisable to conduct DPIAs in relation to projects your company has been involved in for a long time, particularly those towards the riskier end of the spectrum in terms of personal data processing. Examples may include:

- Employee monitoring software.
- Marketing projects involving contacting large numbers of individuals.
- Projects involving collating data from a number of different sources, such as for pricing.

Does the obligation to carry out DPIAs exist against Controller and Processors?

The obligation to conduct DPIAs exists against Controllers. However, when companies act as Processors, they may wish to conduct DPIAs on

[71] Under GDPR article 35, DPIAs are legally required for processing that 'is likely to result in a high risk to the rights and freedoms of natural persons'. GDPR says this is particularly relevant in relation to 'new technologies'.

their own processing activities, even if they are not legally obliged to do so. This can help them demonstrate data protection compliance to their Controller clients. It can also assist Processors in ensuring they comply with GDPR obligations generally.

Can one DPIA cover a multitude of similar projects?

GDPR says 'a single assessment (DPIA) may address a set of similar processing operations that present similar high risks'.[72] You can do one DPIA for a number of projects if the data processing you are doing is similar.

How is the Data Protection Officer involved in DPIAs?

Under GDPR, your company should 'seek the advice of the data protection officer' where there is one in place 'when carrying out a data protection impact assessment'. [73]

What topics should the DPIA cover?

GDPR sets out four subjects that the DPIA must include.[74] The DPIA must include:

1. **A description of the data processing.**
2. **A description of whether the project is necessary and proportionate.**
3. **An assessment of the risks to people posed by the project.**
4. **The steps you have taken to minimise the data protection risks.**

For example, an insurance company wishes to process health data relating to its customers for the purposes of helping set insurance premiums. The

[72] GDPR – Article 35(1)

[73] GDPR – Article 35(2)

[74] GDPR – Article 35(7) (a)-(d)

DPIA sets out the measures taken by the insurance company to minimise the privacy risks to individuals:

a) The insurance company decides to limit the health data it collects to what is absolutely necessary.

b) Further, they only process health data if they have the explicit consent of the customers.

c) Next, they ensure they have appropriate IT Security Controls in place in relation to the health data.

Once the DPIA is finished, do I have to continue to monitor the data processing?

Yes. GDPR says you should review the DPIA particularly where there is any change to the data processing during the lifetime of the project. [75]

Keep your riskier DPIAs under review and go back to look at them to make sure that the team within your business who is responsible for doing the processing is continuing to stay within the rules.

Tracking your DPIAs

You must track your DPIAs carefully. This helps ensure you have:

- Proper records of your DPIAs.
- An understanding of any outstanding tasks on DPIAs.

A very basic example of a tracker template might look like this:

[75] GDPR – Article 35(11)

DPIA Number	Date received	Current status (Pending/ completed)	Summary of issues	Summary of advice given by DPO and date	Date approval was granted	Monitoring – Has the project been monitored to ensure the DPIA recommendations are carried out?

What happens if the DPIA is rejected by the Data Protection Officer but the company wishes to proceed with the project?

It can be risky for a company to override the Data Protection Officer's view on a DPIA. If the company does not agree with the Data Protection Officer's view, then they should record their decision and the reasons for overriding the view of the Data Protection Officer.

When must we ever send a copy of our DPIA to regulators?

Under Article 36 of GDPR 'the controller shall consult the supervisory authority (such as the ICO in the UK) prior to processing where a data protection impact assessment under Article 35 indicates that the processing would result in a high risk in the absence of measures taken by the controller to mitigate the risk'. [76]

[76] GDPR – Article 36(1)

Suggested DPIA form template

In this section, a DPIA template is set out. There is no one correct way to perform a Data Protection Impact Assessment. The form below is quite thorough and is inspired by the ICO template DPIA form although I have changed some of the questions to make the DPIA template below more appropriate to financial services firms.

Remember, how you achieve this in your company is your decision. Feel free to add or remove sections from the DPIA below based on your preferences.

Submitting controller details

Name of controller	
DPIA reference number	
Subject/title of DPO	

1. Describe the processing

• Describe the project and what the project hopes to achieve	
• What type of personal data is being processed?	
• What will the personal data be used for?	
• Is there any profiling or scoring happening?	
• Where will the personal data be stored?	

• How did you collect the personal data?	
• Will the personal data be mixed with other personal data?	
• Will you disclose the personal data to any third parties?	
• Is any of the personal data processing high risk?	

2. Describe the scope of the processing

• Who will have access to the personal data?	
• Is any of the personal data special category personal data?	
• How much data will be processed?	
• How often will it be processed?	
• How long will the personal data be retained?	
• How many individuals will be impacted by this project?	
• Is this a global project?	

3. Describe the context

• Do you have a pre-existing relationship with the individuals e.g. are they customer prospects?	
• Is this project within the reasonable expectation of individuals?	
• Does the project process the personal data of minors or vulnerable people?	
• Is new technology involved?	

4. Describe the purposes of the processing

• What is the project goal?	
• What is the impact on individuals?	
• What are the benefits of the project for the company, individuals or society?	
• Could the aims of the project be achieved without processing the personal data or by processing less personal data?	

5. Consultation process

• Do you need to tell individuals about this project before it starts?	

• What departments within your organisation have you consulted?	
• Do you need to ask your outsourced suppliers or processors about this?	
• Do you plan to consult any experts, for example, lawyers or Information Security?	

6. Assess necessity and proportionality

• How will you stop function creep?	
• How will you make sure you respect the data protection principles, such as not keeping personal data for too long and processing personal data accurately?	
• What information will you give individuals about the project?	
• Will individuals be able to assert their GDPR rights in relation to the data processed as a result of this project?	
• Is any of the personal data transferred internationally?	
• Describe the risks to individuals posed by this project.	

7. Identify measures to reduce risk – To be completed by the DPO

• **Options to reduce risk e.g. setting out technical controls, training, security measures or reduction in the amount of data processed.**	

8. Sign off and record outcomes – To be completed by the DPO

• **Summary of DPO's advice, including on steps required to reduce the risk.**	
• **DPIA Approved or Rejected**	
• **Date**	

Practical steps:

1. Implement a DPIA process in your company and make sure the DPIA template form asks all the right questions.
2. Train the appropriate staff involved in projects and data processing on their DPIA obligations.
3. Ensure your internal staff Data Protection Policy has a section on DPIAs so that DPIAs form part of your company policy.
4. Keep records of all of your DPIAs.

CHAPTER FOUR

DATA PROTECTION AND MARKETING IN FINANCIAL SERVICES

Marketing is crucial in financial services to:

- Build relationships with customers
- Compete with other firms in the marketplace
- Tell customers about your products
- Protect and enhance your company brand

In the old days, marketing was often limited to posting or emailing offers and promotions to customers. Marketing practices have since become increasingly sophisticated. Companies often use data analytics, online tracking and Artificial Intelligence to better understand customer preferences.

This chapter is a quick overview of the Marketing rules in relation to financial services, along with some practical steps that you can take in order to stay compliant.

In many cases, consent is needed to send marketing emails to individuals, such as ordinary customers. On some occasions, you may be able to send marketing emails to personal work email addresses (such as DaveJones@RedInsurance.com) by relying on legitimate interests under GDPR, rather than consent. This is explained in more detail below.

The main direct marketing laws and regulations

In the UK, the main rules on direct marketing appear in:

- UK GDPR
- Data Protection Act 2018 ('DPA 2018')

- The Privacy and Electronic Communications (EC Directive) Regulations 2003. These Regulations are referred to as 'PECR'. PECR still applies post-Brexit. PECR is UK legislation which implements an EU Directive (EU Directive 2002/58/EC). This EU Directive is known as the 'E-Privacy Directive' and it sets out many of the rules on marketing and consent.

The rules in the EU on direct marketing are similar to the UK rules. The EU rules appear in GDPR and EU Directive 2002/58/EC. This chapter largely focuses on the UK requirements.

Recent fines for direct marketing in financial services

Company	Fine	Date	Marketing Breach
1. A pensions company	£45,000	December 2020	The ICO fined a pensions company for making 39,722 connected unsolicited calls for the purposes of direct marketing in relation to occupational pension schemes or personal pension schemes contrary to regulation 21B of PECR.[77]
2. A mortgage and loans broker	£50,000	December 2020	The ICO fined a mortgage and loans broker £50,000 for illegally sending 174,342 nuisance marketing texts.[78]
3. A claims management company	£250,000	October 2020	The ICO fined a claims management company £250,000 for breaking electronic marketing law. During a six-month period,

[77] https://ico.org.uk/action-weve-taken/enforcement/pension-house-exchange-limited/.

[78] https://ico.org.uk/action-weve-taken/enforcement/osl-financial-consultancy-limited/.

			the company made 15.1 million calls in relation to claims management services such as mis-sold PPI. The 1.1 million people who received the calls did not consent to receiving them. [79]
4. Pension provider	£130,000	September 2020	A pension provider was fined £130,000 for making more than 100,000 unauthorised direct marketing calls to people about their pensions.[80]

All of these cases attracted heavy media interest.

What is direct marketing?

Under Section 122(5) of the Data Protection Act 2018, "direct marketing" means *'the communication (by whatever means) of advertising or marketing material which is directed to particular individuals'.*

This includes sending marketing communications to individuals by:

- Phone calls
- Texts
- Emails
- Social media messages

Direct marketing is advertising or marketing material sent to individuals.

There are two elements here. Firstly, it must be advertising or marketing material. Secondly, it must be sent to individuals. We look at these concepts in more detail below.

Advertising or marketing material – If the communication is a service email or a form of communication, such as asking a customer to update

[79] https://ico.org.uk/action-weve-taken/enforcement/reliance-advisory-limited/.

[80] https://ico.org.uk/action-weve-taken/enforcement/cps-advisory-ltd-mpn/

their account details, then it is not caught by the marketing rules. However, companies must be careful here. If there is **any** marketing material within the email or communication, then it is a marketing communication.

Sometimes, companies try to disguise marketing emails by putting marketing information into service emails. For example, they might send an email saying "Dear Mr Smith, Please update your account details for our records. Please note, we are also offering 15% off our Home Insurance Policies in January". This is a marketing email and it is therefore subject to all the rules on marketing.

Similarly, the ICO has said a company "cannot avoid the direct marketing rules by labelling its message as a survey or market research if it is actually trying to sell goods or services, or to collect data to help it (or others) to contact people for marketing purposes at a later date". This is sometimes referred to as 'sugging'. [81]

Individuals – If the communication is not sent to an individual, then it is not direct marketing and is therefore not subject to the rules on marketing. For example, if a marketing email is sent to an email address not related to an individual such as info@bankofireland.com then that email is not subject to the rules on direct marketing and consents.

GDPR – What should I remember about GDPR when our company is sending Direct Marketing communications?

GDPR regulates the processing of personal data. This includes sending marketing communications to individual consumers and also individuals at their personal work email addresses such as Mary.Smithee@RedInsurance.com.

GDPR considerations in relation to marketing:

1. **People have a right to say they no longer wish to receive marketing material** -This is known as the Right to Opt Out of Marketing[82].

[81] ICO – Direct Marketing Guidance – Para 39, 3 June 2018

[82] GDPR – Article 21(2)

Sometimes, customers say that they do not wish to receive any more marketing material. They may do so by clicking an unsubscribe button at the foot of the email. Alternatively, they may send an email saying that they do not wish to receive any more marketing information. If you do receive such a communication from a customer, then you must take it seriously. You will be in breach of the person's GDPR right to opt out of marketing if you continue to market to them. This could put your company at risk of fines or litigation.

2. **Privacy Notices** – Customers should be told about how their personal information is used for marketing purposes in your Privacy Notices (such as your company Website Privacy Policy). You should set this out simply and clearly. You should tell customers in Privacy Notices about the marketing communications you may send them. You should tell them about any data sharing or selling you are doing for marketing purposes (consent is also likely to be needed for these).[83] See Chapter 12 for more details on Privacy Notices.

3. **Profiling** – Companies engage in profiling when they record or analyse customer behaviour or characteristics. Sometimes, the profiles that companies build on individual customers are used for marketing purposes.

   For example, Big Insurance decides to build profiles of 1,000 of their customers. The profile is a record of each customer's age, job, address, income and claims history. Big Insurance use the profiles of each customer to help them decide which types of marketing to send to each of them. This allows Big Insurance to send more targeted marketing to their customers.

   When a company does engage in profiling for the purposes of marketing, they should:

---

[83] GDPR – Articles 13 and 14

- Tell the customer about this in the Privacy Notice.
- Give the customer the right to opt out of that profiling, by allowing them to contact you and have their details removed from the profiling database.[84]

4. **Lawful basis** – Anytime you send marketing to an individual, then you must have a lawful basis in place. If you do not have the individual's consent, then you must have a legitimate interest to market to them.

Specific Rules on Sending Marketing information to Individuals

A. Email Marketing

The rules on email marketing are complicated so you might have to read them more than once.

Individual subscribers such as consumers

This section sets out the rules on sending emails to 'individual subscribers', such as the customers of a bank.

The rules on email marketing to individuals such as customers are set out in Regulation 22 of PECR.

Regulation 22 says that companies must have received the prior opt in consent of individuals before sending marketing emails.[85]

In other words, people must tick a box or do something active in order to agree to marketing. You cannot assume they want to receive your marketing information.

There is an exception to this. This is known as the 'Soft Opt-In Rule'. The rules say that prior opt in consent for emails is not needed if:

- **Sale** – You obtained the customer's email address in the course of a sale or negotiation for a sale.

---

[84] GDPR – Article 21(2)

[85] PECR – Regulation 22(2)

- **Similar products** – The marketing relates to similar products or services.
- **Opt Out** – The person is given the chance to unsubscribe from receiving further emails. [86]

Example 1:

- Big Bank want to tell a customer called Judy about a new offer on low interest loans.
- Judy has been making enquiries about low interest loans.
- Judy has been a Big Bank customer for ten years.
- Big Bank do not have Judy's explicit consent, but they rely on the 'Soft Opt-In Rule'.
- Big Bank put an 'unsubscribe from further emails' link at the bottom of the email so that Judy can opt out in future if she so wishes.

Example 2:

- Big Bank purchase personal data from a list broker.
- The data purchased includes the personal email address of Reggie Hammond.
- Big Bank do not have any prior relationship with Reggie.
- Big Bank want to send marketing emails promoting low interest loans to their marketing contacts and customers.
- Big Bank are unable to send Reggie the promotional email because Reggie has not given consent.
- Big Bank are unable to rely on the 'Soft Opt-In Rule'.

[86] PECR – Regulation 22(3) for the UK/ E-Privacy Directive – Article 13 for the EU

Sending marketing emails to personal corporate email addresses such as Dave.Jones@RedInsurance.com.

The rules for sending emails to corporate subscribers are different. Corporate subscribers include sending emails to personal corporate email addresses like Dave.Jones@RedInsurance.com.

Prior opt-in consent is not always needed in this case.

However, GDPR still does apply to sending these kinds of emails to personal corporate email addresses.

Companies sending marketing emails to personal corporate email addresses must:

- Tell the person who they are.[87]
- Give the person the chance to unsubscribe from receiving further emails.[88]
- Have a legal basis for sending the promotional email under GDPR, such as legitimate interests. [89]

Sending marketing emails to personal corporate email addresses such as Dave.Jones@RedInsurance.com. Can we rely on legitimate interest?

Recital 47 of GDPR says that direct marketing may be a legitimate interest. However, companies must be careful to ensure that they have a good, solid argument to rely on legitimate interests in each case.

The ICO says '*You can rely on legitimate interests for marketing activities if you can show the way you use people's data is proportionate, has a minimal privacy impact, and people would not be surprised or likely to object to what you are doing – but only if you don't need consent under PECR.*'[90]

---

[87] PECR – Regulation 23

[88] GDPR – Article 21

[89] GDPR – Article 6

[90] https://ico.org.uk/for-organisations/in-your-sector/marketing/the-rules-around-business-to-business-marketing-the-gdpr-and-pecr/.

In other words, you need to decide whether relying on legitimate interests is appropriate before using this lawful basis.

For example:

- Big Bank want to send a marketing email to Davey's work email address at Davey.Jones@RedInsurance.com.
- Big Bank do not require prior opt in consent to send the marketing email.
- However, sending marketing information to the work email address is subject to the rules under GDPR.
- Under GDPR, Big Bank must tell Davey who they are and give him the chance to unsubscribe from further emails.
- Big Bank also need a legal basis to send Davey the marketing email such as 'consent' or 'legitimate interest'.
- Big Bank are confident they can rely on legitimate interests to send Davey the email.
- They are confident Davey would not be surprised or likely to object to receiving their email because they have had a relationship with Davey in the past.
- Big Bank record the legitimate interest decision they took in their records so they have it in case Davey ever complains about receiving the email.

B. Texts, emails and social media messages

The same rules above for emails are repeated for messages sent via text, SMS and social media messages, such as direct messages sent via Twitter or Linkedin.[91]

[91] PECR – Regulation 2(1)

C. Sending pre-recorded messages by phone

Consent is always needed to call numbers in order to send pre-recorded direct marketing voice messages.

For example, Big Bank want to send a pre-recorded voice message to James' work phone number. Big Bank need the prior opt in consent of James to do this.[92]

D. Live phone calls

Live phone calls to individual subscribers such as consumers

It is possible to call a consumer to market to them if:

- The person has not previously said 'no' to receiving such calls, and
- The person has not told the Telephone Preference Service that they object to receiving such calls.

Companies are legally required to check with the Telephone Preference Service ('TPS') to see if a person has objected to receiving such calls. If the person has objected to receiving them, then you should not call them.

For example:

- Big Bank decide to call Deirdre to tell her about some promotional offers.
- Big Bank check their records to ensure Deirdre has not opted out of such marketing.
- Big Bank also check with the TPS to see if Deirdre has ever told the TPS that she does not want to receive such calls.
- Big Bank are confident that Deirdre has not told Big Bank or the TPS that she does not want to receive such calls.
- Big Bank are also confident there is a legitimate interest in place under GDPR that would allow Big Bank to make the call to

[92] PECR – Regulation 19

Deirdre because Deirdre would reasonably expect to receive the call.

Claims Management Services and **Pension Schemes** do need the consent of the person before making live marketing calls.[93]

Live phone calls to corporate subscribers such as individuals working in a company

It is possible to call an individual in a company to market to them if:

- They have not previously said 'no' to receiving such calls and
- They have not told the Corporate Telephone Preference Service ('CTPS') that they object to receiving such calls. [94] [95]

Companies are legally required to check with the Corporate Telephone Preference Service to see if a person has objected to receiving such calls.[96]

However, if you are marketing claims management services or pension schemes then you do need consent.

If we are relying on consent to market then what kind of consent is needed?

We have set out above the requirements in relation to when consents are needed for marketing. But what kinds of consents are needed in order to send marketing information and what should those consents look like?

Firstly, PECR applies the GDPR standard of consent.

---

[93] https://ico.org.uk/for-organisations/guide-to-pecr/electronic-and-telephone-marketing/telephone-marketing/.

[94] PECR – Regulation 21

[95] ICO Guidance – Direct Marketing – Page 39 – 3 June 2018

[96] Privacy and Electronic Communications (EC Directive) Regulations 2004

Under GDPR and PECR consent [97]must be:

- **Freely given** – You cannot tell a customer that they must consent or make your services conditional on them consenting. [98]

- **Specific** – It should be granular. You should not hide the consent in a lot of other terms and conditions.[99]

- **Informed** – You should give the person enough information so they can make their choice. You should advise them that they can withdraw their consent if they want.[100]

- **Clear and plain** – Keep it clear so the person knows what they are consenting to.[101]

- **Affirmative** – The person must actively do something such as ticking a box or saying 'yes' to something to show their consent. You cannot take their consent for granted by ticking the box for the customer.[102]

Your company should keep records of the consents you rely on.[103]

Individuals can withdraw their consent at any time.[104] If you are relying on their consent to market to them and they withdraw their consent, then you must cease marketing to them.

---

[97] GDPR – Article 4(11)

[98] GDPR – Article 7(4)

[99] GDPR – Article 7(2)

[100] GDPR – Article 4(11)

[101] GDPR – Article 7(2)

[102] GDPR – Article 4(11)

[103] GDPR – Article 7(1)

[104] GDPR – Article 7(3)

Practical steps

1. **Audit your marketing department** – Carry out a Data Protection Audit of your marketing department. Send out questionnaires and have meetings to find out:

    - Who they are marketing to e.g. customers, clients prospects
    - What privacy notices these individuals receive
    - Whether the consents they rely on are sufficient
    - What kind of training the marketing department receive
    - Where they obtain their marketing information e.g. internally or from list brokers
    - How long is the marketing information retained for
    - Whether telephone numbers are checked against Do Not Call lists made by the Telephone Preference Service

    Asking the difficult questions of your marketing department now can help prevent problems from happening with Regulators and customers later on down the road.

2. **System** – Put an electronic system in place so you know which individuals have consented to receiving marketing material from your company. Ensure this system can record the details of consents received from customers as you may need to produce the consent to a Regulator at a later stage. The system should also record withdrawals of consent from customers.

3. **Data Protection Impact Assessment** – Ask your marketing department to complete a Data Protection Impact Assessment (See Chapter3), for new Marketing campaigns and initiatives. You can risk assess these campaigns and ensure they stay on the right side of the rules.

4. **Training the marketing department** – Train your marketing department regularly, perhaps twice a year, on the rules in

relation to marketing. Give them a general overview and break the rules down for them on consents, legitimate interests and the right to opt out of marketing.

5. **Marketing Policy** – You may wish to put a Data Protection and Marketing Policy in place in your company. The policy should set out the rules in terms of the types of marketing that is permitted by your company.

CHAPTER FIVE

HOW GDPR IMPACTS KNOW YOUR CUSTOMER CHECKS

Introduction

According to the United Nations, the amount of money estimated to be laundered globally each year is 2 – 5% of global GDP, or $2 trillion in US dollars. [105] Companies must guard against any customers who may be trying to use their services to commit crimes.

Companies must check out their customers before doing business with them. These are often referred to as Know Your Customer or 'KYC' checks. Companies must ensure they conduct these checks in a manner that is consistent with GDPR. This chapter outlines some of the responsibilities on KYC checks.

What is Know Your Customer (KYC)?

Know Your Customer (sometimes referred to as Know Your Client) is the process by which companies:

- Check the identity of customers, and
- Assess their details to make sure they are not using your company to do anything dodgy such as laundering money, committing fraud or financing terrorists.

These KYC checks are usually done when a customer is being 'onboarded' i.e. at the beginning of their relationship with the financial services company. Further KYC checks may be done at various stages in the relationship, such as when a bank customer wants to make a large cash deposit.

---

[105] https://www.unodc.org/unodc/en/money-laundering/overview.html.

Examples of KYC checks

Companies perform many different types of KYC checks. For example:

- **Anti-money laundering** – Clive is opening a bank account with Big Bank. He arrives at his local branch with £20,000 cash in a suitcase. Anti-money laundering checks must be done before Clive can open the account and deposit the money.

- **Fraud** – Robert has a house insurance policy with Grimm Home Insurance and he wishes to make a claim against the policy. He states the garage at his home has burnt down and that it was worth £100,000. His story has many inconsistencies. Grimm want to conduct checks on Robert's data whilst investigating the claim to ensure no fraud is taking place.

- **Counter terrorist financing** – John wishes to transfer £50,000 to individuals in a remote country. He tells his bank, Solid Bank, that the individuals are friends of his and that the money is a 'Christmas present'. Solid Bank have suspicions about John and the recipients of the money. They wish to conduct checks on this proposed transaction to make sure no counter-terrorist financing is taking place.

Before conducting these checks, the financial services firm usually asks the customer to complete a form. The form usually asks the customer for their details and proof of their identity, such as a passport.

Some tips for complying with the Data Protection Principles when conducting KYC checks

As we discussed in Chapter 1, when we process personal data, we must ensure this is done in accordance with the Data Protection Principles. Following the Data Protection Principles is the best way of ensuring your company is compliant with GDPR.

These principles are set out at Article 5 of GDPR.

Below are some examples on how to comply with the Data Protection Principles when conducting KYC checks:

1. **Lawfulness, fairness and transparency** – Be open with your customers in privacy policies and customer notices. Set out how and why personal data is processed for the purposes of conducting KYC checks.

2. **Purpose limitation** – Don't collect KYC data and then go behind the customer's back to use it for an entirely different purpose.

3. **Data minimisation** – Do not collect more KYC data than you need and ensure customers are not asked questions on KYC forms that are over and above what is necessary.

4. **Accuracy** – Review the sources of your information that you use to conduct your KYC checks to ensure the data is accurate and up to date. Make sure no poor quality or out-of-date data is used to perform KYC checks on customers because this could lead to unfair outcomes for the customer.

5. **Storage limitation** – Know Your Customer records should not be kept for longer than is necessary.

   This is a challenge where KYC rules are concerned because many laws and regulations impacting KYC checks (such as Terrorist Financing and Transfer of Funds (Information on the Payer) Regulations 2017) mandate that certain data is retained for a specified period.

   Firms should draw up Data Retention Schedules to set out how long personal data relating to KYC checks is to be retained.

6. **Security** – KYC data can be very sensitive and it could get your company in trouble if it fell into the wrong hands, particularly as it could include data related to criminal offences. Make sure there are good security controls around this data. In particular, use good technical controls such as encryption. Also, make sure there are good access controls to ensure that only the staff who need to

see the KYC data can access it. See Chapter 9 for more details on Security.

7. **Accountability** – Keep appropriate records in place of the KYC checks you conduct, in case there is ever a complaint made to the ICO about the data processing you conduct when performing KYC checks.

Legal bases for KYC checks under Article 6 of GDPR

As we explained in Chapter 1, all data processing requires a legal basis.

Whenever a company processes personal data for KYC, it must have a legal basis in place under GDPR to do so.

The legal bases for processing personal data are set out at Article 6 of GDPR.

The legal bases most relevant to KYC checks appear below:

a) **Consent of the data subject** – Be careful when using this as a legal basis to conduct Know Your Customer Checks. Consent[106] might not always be the most appropriate basis, particularly if you have a legal obligation under another law, such as an anti-money laundering law to perform the KYC checks. If you do wish to rely on consent, then it must be opt-in consent. In other words, you must allow the customer to consent themselves. You cannot pre-tick the box for the customer. See Chapter 1 for more details.

b) **Necessary to comply with a Legal Obligation** – Processing is necessary for compliance with a legal obligation to which the controller is subject.[107] This may often be an appropriate legal basis for KYC checks. Remember that to rely on this ground, your company must have a legal obligation to do something and not a legal choice or discretion. Some laws may oblige your

[106] GDPR – Article 6(1)(a)

[107] GDPR – Article 6(1)(c)

company to conduct checks on a customer for an anti-money laundering purpose. Check these laws carefully before relying on them to conduct KYC checks.

c) **Necessary for the Legitimate interest of your firm** –This is where the processing is necessary for the purposes of the legitimate interests pursued by the controller or by a third party[108]. Legitimate interests may be an appropriate legal basis to rely on for conducting customer checks if there is no legal obligation (see b. above).

   For example, an insurance company may think that one of their customers is trying to defraud them by making a false claim. There is no legal obligation to conduct fraud checks here so the insurance company may be able to rely on legitimate interests. After all, an insurance company should have a legitimate interest in preventing customers from trying to defraud them.

It is up to you to judge which legal basis is most appropriate in the circumstances based on the kinds of KYC you are doing.

For example, Top Bank want to carry out anti-money laundering (AML) checks on David, one of their new customers because David wishes to open an account and to lodge £500,000 in cash. Top Bank's Compliance Officer advises that a specific AML law is in place that mandates that Top Bank conduct certain checks on David. Top Bank want also to comply with GDPR. Top Bank consider asking David for his **Consent** to conduct the AML checks but it also considers relying on **Legitimate Interests** to conduct the AML checks. Top Bank decide that **Legal Obligation** is the most appropriate basis to rely on in this case to conduct the AML checks on David. They believe this is a more appropriate legal basis than Consent or Legitimate Interests.

See Chapter 1 for more details on legal bases.

---

[108] GDPR – Article 6(1)(f)

Special category personal data

If you are processing special category data to conduct the KYC checks, such as personal data relating to race or ethnicity, then you will need a legal basis set out at Article 6 of GDPR (see paragraph above) and an additional legal basis under Article 9 of GDPR. Check the Article 9 conditions carefully to ensure one of them applies before processing any special category personal data. The most common Article 9 conditions for KYC checks may be 'explicit consent' or 'substantial public interest' but you must check carefully to see if they are appropriate.

It is legally complex to process special category data so you should first ask yourself whether you can achieve the same goal without processing the special category data.

See Chapter 1 for more details.

Criminal personal data

There are rules in place around processing of personal data relating to criminal convictions and offences and alleged offences [109] ('criminal data').

For example, if a bank or insurance company carries out checks on whether a person has criminal convictions as part of their fraud or AML checks, then they are processing criminal personal data.

As with special category data, it is legally complex to process criminal data so you should first ask yourself whether you can achieve the same goal without processing the criminal data.

Firstly, you must still have a lawful basis for your processing under Article 6. (See 'The legal bases for processing personal data under Article 6' above).

Secondly, you must also have an appropriate Data Protection Act 2018 Schedule 1 condition to process the criminal data.

[109] Data Protection Act 2018 – Section 11(2)

The Schedule 1 conditions that might be most appropriate in financial services for processing criminal data are:

- Preventing or detecting unlawful acts
- Protecting the public against dishonesty
- Preventing fraud
- Suspicion of terrorist financing or money laundering
- Consent
- Legal claims
- Insurance

If you are going to process criminal personal data, then you should refer to Schedule 1, Part 1 of paragraphs 1-37 of the Data Protection Act 2018 in the UK to check that the conditions apply to you.

See Chapter 1 for more details.

Privacy Notices

Companies must tell customers about how their data is processed in Privacy Notices. This includes information about how data is processed for the purposes of KYC checks.

For example, Green Bank has received an application to open an account from Santosh. Green Bank will be performing KYC checks on Santosh's data. This includes checking Santosh's data against their fraud databases to see if Santosh has ever been alleged to have committed fraud. Green Bank want to be open with Santosh about the kinds of checks they conduct. They tell customers about the KYC checks they will be performing in their online Privacy Policy. They also include a short Privacy Notice at the top of the customer application form. These notices explain how Santosh's data will be processed. They also explain the details of the KYC checks that will be performed.

See Chapter 12 for more details on Privacy Notices.

Automated decision making

Sometimes companies use computer software to carry out KYC checks on individuals. When companies do this, they need to make sure the software operates in a way that is consistent with GDPR.

There are rules under GDPR on:

- **Computer decision making** – Making decisions about individuals by computer alone (without any human involvement), and
- **Profiling** – Building profiles of individuals to make assessments about them.[110]

To make a decision about a person using a computer or to conduct profiling on a person, then the processing must be:

- **Contract** – Necessary for the entry into or performance of a contract; or
- **Authorised by Law** – Authorised by domestic law applicable to the controller; or
- **Explicit Consent** – Based on the individual's explicit consent.[111]

Make sure your KYC checks comply with the law on automated processing or profiling. Build in ways to allow people to challenge the decision of the computer, such as through asking a human being to review the decision to ensure that it is not unfair.

For example, Big Bank receive applications to open accounts from 100 customers. Big Bank use a computer program to scan all of the applications. The computer program is processing the customer data to see if any of the individuals have been involved in fraud in the past. The computer tells Big Bank that 5 of the customers have been involved in fraudulent activity. The computer does not allow these 5 customers to

[110] GDPR Article 22(1)

[111] GDPR – Article 22(2)

open an account. In order to ensure the process is fair, Big Bank ask one of their employees to review the computer decisions. Big Bank want to make sure there is some human review of the computer's decision, to ensure customers are treated fairly.

Data Protection Impact Assessment (DPIA)

If a company is starting a new project, to conduct KYC checks, then they should complete a Data Protection Impact Assessment (DPIA) form. For example, Big Insurance decide to roll out new computer software to conduct KYC checks on customers before they can purchase an insurance policy. Big Insurance complete a Data Protection Impact Assessment form so they can mitigate some of the risks around the personal data processing.

See Chapter 3 for more details on DPIAs.

Recap of the Chapter and Practical Steps

1. **Retention Periods** – Set out time limits for how long you intend to keep your KYC data.

2. **Accuracy** – Make sure any data you rely on to perform KYC checks is accurate and up to date. For example, if you run your customer names against a fraud database, then you should check to ensure this data is accurate.

3. **Security** – Work with your IT Security Teams to ensure there is appropriate security in place around your KYC data, to prevent it from being hacked or compromised. KYC data can be very sensitive and you must ensure it does not fall into the wrong hands. Proper encryption and access controls should be in place to stop this data from falling into the wrong hands.

4. **Privacy Notices** – You must tell customers about the KYC checks you are conducting in your Privacy Policy. Place a short notice at the top of the KYC form, explaining why KYC data is collected and used and refer the customer to the full Privacy Policy, if they want more details.

5. **DPIAs** – Conduct a Data Protection Impact Assessment form for any KYC data processing that is potentially risky including:

    - Using new KYC software
    - Hiring a vendor to help you with KYC data
    - Processing special category data or criminal data for the purposes of KYC

6. **Software** – If you are using software to perform KYC checks, you should make sure the computer program treats customer fairly. For example, you may wish to ensure there is human involvement in the decision-making process.

CHAPTER SIX

USING THE CLOUD IN FINANCIAL SERVICES

The cloud in financial services

The cloud is a necessity in financial services. According to Gartner, "worldwide end-user spending on public cloud services is forecast to grow 18.4% in 2021 to total $304.9 billion, up from $257.5 billion in 2020".[112]

Cloud solutions are important. For example, they help financial services companies to:

- Store and access customer data
- Process staff data
- Put better security in place around their data
- Integrate different parts of the group

What is the cloud?

The cloud – The ICO defines cloud computing "*as access to computing resources, on demand, via a network.*"[113] In other words, the cloud allows you to access data via the internet rather than having to access data that is being stored on your computer.

[112] Gartner Forecasts Worldwide Public Cloud End-User Spending to Grow 18% in 2021 – Press Release November 2020.

[113] ICO's 'Guidance on the Use of Cloud Computing' page 3. Please note this document predates GDPR although many of the concepts are still relevant.

Cloud provider – *"A cloud provider is a company that delivers cloud computing based services and solutions to businesses and/or individuals."*[114] [115] The cloud provider provides the hardware and software elements for the cloud customer's needs.

Cloud customer – A cloud customer is the company (or individual) that contracts with the cloud provider for particular cloud services.

Types of cloud

There are a number of different types of cloud:

Public cloud – The public cloud is where the cloud provider makes the cloud services available to anyone who wants to use them. Amazon Web Services (AWS) and Microsoft Azure are examples of public cloud deployments. The public cloud allows companies to access data via the internet.

Private cloud – This is a cloud environment that the cloud provider only makes available to particular company or user.

Community cloud – This is where a cloud environment is shared by a number of cloud customers with similar needs.

For a fictional example, Green Cloud offer a community cloud service that is specifically tailored to some of their Insurance Cloud customers. The Insurance Cloud customers have similar security needs. The insurance companies who use this service like it because they find it less expensive than the Private Cloud but find it meets their specific needs as insurers

Hybrid cloud – A hybrid cloud infrastructure is where companies mix public and private clouds. Most large financial services companies will use a combination of different types of cloud.

---

[114] Techopedia.com – What does Cloud Provider Mean

[115] Gartner Says Worldwide IaaS Public Cloud Services Market Grew 37.3% in 2019 – Press Release – August 2020

Types of cloud services

Infrastructure as a Service (IaaS) – This is the most basic type of cloud service. It will provide you with the basic infrastructure, such as the use of the cloud provider's hardware.

Platform as a service (Paas) – This is where you use a cloud provider's computer platform as a base. You use that base for your own software applications.

Software as a service (SaaS) – This is where a company pays a cloud provider for access to a complete software application which the cloud customer accesses. Most of the work is done for the company by the cloud provider. The company does not need to install or to manage the software on their own devices as it is done remotely by the cloud provider. The company has full access to all of the software services. The cloud provider can update and store the software themselves.

Cloud providers – Controllers or Processors?

You will recall from Chapter 1 that:

- A Controller determines the how and why of the personal data processing.
- A Processor processes personal data on behalf of the Controller.

In most cases, cloud providers will be Processors.

You must be careful when dealing with cloud providers that they do not 'push the envelope' in respect of how they process personal data. Sometimes, cloud providers look to act autonomously with the data they process on your behalf. For example, they may wish to use the data for their own purposes such as data analytics or data selling. This could turn the cloud provider into a Controller.

There can be risks in allowing a cloud provider autonomy over your data. It lessens the control you have over your data. It is best to ensure your cloud providers are Processors who are subject to strict contractual obligations.

Using the cloud in financial services – Avoiding the risks

Risk mitigation 1 – Understanding your cloud usage

Cloud usage touches many aspects of a company's operations. There are likely to be numerous cloud providers assisting your company with marketing, IT, human resources, customer management and many other functions.

Untangling your cloud usage can be complex. It is advisable to try to get a better handle on the cloud providers your company is using to see if there are any gaps in place.

There may be a register of cloud providers already in existence held by your company IT department that can help you with this.

You may wish to put a table together to help give you a basic understanding of your cloud usage.

It might look something like this:

Cloud provider:	White Cloud
Date cloud provider was onboarded:	2008
Due Diligence done on the cloud provider?	No
Personal data processed:	This Software as a Service application allows us to manage customer purchase information.
Has DPIA been done to risk assess this cloud provider?	No
Is there a contract in place?	Very limited contract with no GDPR processor clauses.
Areas of risk or concern:	Large amount of sensitive customer data. Insufficient contract and no due diligence or risk assessment .
Next steps:	Amend contract to include GDPR clauses. Perform DPIA.

This can help you understand where your compliance risks are.

Risk mitigation 2 – Perform a Data Protection Impact Assessment (DPIA)

In Chapter 3, we discussed Data Protection Impact Assessment (DPIA).

I would advise carrying out a DPIA when:

- You onboard a new cloud provider.
- You are using an existing cloud provider and no DPIA was done when they were onboarded.
- Your existing cloud provider has changed the way in which they process your personal data.

DPIAs are a useful tool for identifying and mitigating risks ahead of time.

See Chapter 3 for more details on DPIAs.

Risk mitigation 3 – Cloud Policy

You must ensure your company is operating in sync with other departments in respect of cloud usage.

Often, a financial services company will have different departments operating independently in respect of their cloud usage.

For example, the Procurement Team may onboard a cloud provider without checking with IT Security or the Data Protection Officer as to whether the cloud services they are using are secure and compliant with laws and regulations, such as GDPR.

You should have an internal Cloud Policy in place that lays down rules in respect of the cloud. The policy should include rules on:

- Selecting and approving a new cloud provider
- Performing a Data Protection Impact Assessment (DPIA) form on the new cloud provider

- Obtaining the approval of the company IT Security Team in respect of cloud services
- Putting an appropriate contract in place with the new cloud provider
- Monitoring the cloud provider throughout the duration of the contract
- Training staff on using cloud services and applications

Risk Mitigation 4 – Selecting cloud providers

Under GDPR, when you select a Processor, you must ensure you *"use only processors providing sufficient guarantees"*[116] that they will keep your personal data safe.

In other words, you must do due diligence on the cloud providers you want to use BEFORE they are onboarded.

Your company should have a process in place to vet cloud providers before they are onboarded.

You should send them a written questionnaire to ask them questions to satisfy yourself that the cloud provider:

- **Expertise** – Has enough expertise to keep your personal data safe.
- **Security** – Has a Privacy and Security Program in place. They should provide you with copies of their Data Protection Policy and Information Security Policy.
- **A good reputation** – Has a good track record in keeping data safe. Check online and with the provider themselves to see if they were ever involved in a privacy breach.

[116] GDPR – Article 28(1)

- **Certifications** – Have certifications that highlight their proficiency in respect of security e.g. ISO 27001.

There are more details on this in Chapter 10 – Third Parties.

Risk Mitigation 5 – Putting contracts in place with the cloud provider

Under GDPR, Controllers must put contracts in place with Processors that are processing personal data on their behalf.

These contracts must contain a specific set of clauses. The clauses put certain obligations on the Processor to process the personal data safely and in accordance with the law.

As we discussed earlier in this chapter, cloud providers are usually Processors. When you use a Processor Cloud Provider, you must include these clauses in your contract with the Processor Cloud Provider. If you do not include these clauses in your contract with the cloud provider, then you are going to be in breach of Article 28 of GDPR. In theory, breach of Article 28 of GDPR can attract a fine of up to 10million or 2% of the global annual turnover of your company.[117]

Article 28 of GDPR sets out the contractual clauses that are required between the Controller and the Processor.

If you do not have these contracts in place with the cloud provider, then your company will be very exposed, particularly if the cloud provider loses or misuses any of the personal data. The contract is your insurance policy against this. It may not cover you for all of the loss and damage you may experience (for example, a contract will not usually cover you against the cost of fines or regulator action caused by the cloud provider's negligence) but it will go some way towards helping to keep your personal data safe.

[117] GDPR – Article 83(4)(a)

What clauses must I include in the contract?

GDPR says that any time a Controller hires a Processor, such as a cloud provider, then it must include the following clauses:[118]

a) **What data is being processed?**

b) **How long the contract with the cloud provider will last?**

c) **The reason for using the cloud provider.**

d) **The type of personal data involved** – For example, customer names, bank account numbers and credit card numbers.

e) **The types of people** – The categories of data subject, for example, customers, employees etc.

f) **The rights and obligations of your company.**

g) **Instructions** – For example, that the cloud provider processor must only act on your instructions.

h) **Cloud provider's employees** – The cloud provider will ensure their employees keep the data confidential.

i) **Security** – The Processor must take appropriate security steps in relation to the data processing.

j) **Cloud provider using sub-processors** – For example, if the cloud provider uses another company to help them to process the data, then they must get consent from your company. You should ask the cloud provider to make available copies of the contracts they have in place with sub-processors who are processing personal data on their behalf. Cloud providers are starting to publish a list of the companies that they are using as sub-processors, as they believe this is a good and more efficient way of getting written authorisation from their Processor clients, instead of writing to each one individually and asking for written authorisation in each case.

[118] GDPR – Article 28

k) **The Cloud provider must help you with GDPR Access and Erasure Requests.** For example, if a customer of your firm makes an Access Request under GDPR and some of the data is on the cloud provider's system, then the cloud provider must provide you with the data so that you can send it on to your customer.

l) **The Cloud provider must help you if there has been a data breach.** For example, if there is a data breach, then the cloud provider has lost your customer data and you have a responsibility to report this matter to a regulator. The cloud provider must help you ascertain the facts so that you can make the report (See Chapter 10 for more details).

m) **Cloud provider must return data** – The cloud provider must delete or return all personal data to the Controller at the end of the contract.

n) **Cloud provider must submit to audits and inspections** – The cloud provider must submit to audits and inspections.

As you can see, there are a lot of clauses your company must include when doing business with Cloud Providers. See Chapter 10 – Contracts for more details.

Your Legal Team should ensure these clauses appear in contracts with cloud providers.

What happens when the cloud provider won't sign these clauses?

Often, the cloud provider may be a huge, multi-national tech company. Under GDPR, they are likely to be a Processor when providing cloud services and your company is likely to be a Controller. However, they may be a very powerful Processor that is used to getting their own way, in relation to contract terms and conditions.

Indeed, they may offer their services on a "take it or leave it" basis. In other words, they may say that you must sign their terms and conditions if you want to use their services. This is all well and good if the terms and conditions they wish you to sign include the GDPR clauses a) – (n) in the paragraph above.

But what if those terms and conditions do NOT include the clauses from (a) – (n) in the paragraph above?

Does this get you off the hook with GDPR? In other words, if the cloud provider is a Processor who won't agree to the GDPR clauses, will you be able to say that you had no choice? No. GDPR places obligations on you to ensure these clauses are in place with any Processor you use, no matter how powerful that Processor is. If a cloud provider refuses to have GDPR clauses in place, then your company is taking a risk in terms of your GDPR compliance and it is up to your company to decide whether it wishes to accept that risk.

Risk Mitigation 6 – Transferring data outside the EEA

We live in a truly global world. When you use a cloud provider, you are entrusting them with your personal data. Many cloud providers process personal data across the globe. They may also use sub-processors who process the personal data in various countries around the world.

When you use a cloud provider, you must ensure:

- You understand where in the world they may be sending your personal data.
- There are mechanisms such as Standard Contractual Clauses in place to allow the transfer of the personal data to a third country. Standard Contractual Clauses are contractual clauses that allow a Controller in the UK or EU to transfer personal data to a Processor (such as a cloud provider) in a third country, such as the United States.

We have covered this subject already in Chapter 2.

Make sure that your legal team has a good idea about where the cloud providers are processing your personal data.

If there are any gaps regarding your transfers, then make sure you have a valid mechanism that allows you to transfer data to a cloud provider in a third country, such as Standard Contractual Clauses.

Risk Mitigation 7 – Reporting data breaches

Under GDPR, your company has certain responsibilities to report some personal data breaches to customers and regulators depending on the seriousness of the breach. Breaches must be reported to regulators "within 72 hours".[119]

If a cloud provider is processing personal data on your behalf and they cause a breach involving this personal data, then they must advise you of this breach without undue delay. [120]

If cloud providers don't tell you about breaches when they occur, then they could get you in trouble with regulators or your own customers.

Make sure the contract with the cloud provider sets out the cloud provider's obligation to tell you about personal data breaches that occur.

Risk mitigation 8 – Security, security, security

Security is the lynchpin of GDPR. We have obligations to have appropriate security in place with any cloud providers with whom we share personal data.

Under Article 32 of GDPR, we are expected to have a level of security in place that is appropriate to the risk relating to the personal data.

When you do entrust a cloud provider to process your personal data, then it is advisable that your IT Security Team weighs in on whether the security controls proposed by the cloud provider in respect of your personal data are sufficient. For example, your IT Security Team might ask if the cloud provider is:

- Using appropriate encryption[121]

---

[119] GDPR – Article 33(1)

[120] GDPR – Article 33(2)

[121] GDPR – Article 32(1)(a)

- Able to keep their systems secure[122]
- Able to restore access to data in the event of systems failing temporarily[123]
- Conducting pen testing to ensure the security of their systems[124]

Check that your IT Security Teams are content with the security controls that will be provided by the Cloud Provider.

Practical steps to take:

1. **Existing cloud providers** – Try and get an understanding of your existing usage of cloud providers.
2. **Cloud Policy** – Put a Cloud Policy in place that sets out the process for engaging cloud providers. Make sure IT Security have oversight of the hiring of any cloud providers so they are happy from a security point of view.
3. **Due Diligence** – Perform appropriate Due Diligence with any cloud provider, before allowing them to work with your company and keep a record of the Due Diligence.
4. **Contract Clauses** – Make sure your cloud provider processors have the appropriate GDPR clauses in place.
5. **Data Protection Impact Assessment (DPIA)** – Ensure all engagements with cloud providers are subject to a DPIA.

[122] GDPR – Article 32(1)(b)

[123] GDPR – Article 32(1)(c)

[124] GDPR – Article 32(1)(d)

CHAPTER SEVEN
BUYING CUSTOMER DATA

Why do Financial Services companies buy personal data?

Companies in financial services may buy personal data for a host of different reasons. For example:

1. **Marketing** – Companies may buy personal data to send individuals marketing information about their products and services.
2. **Risk Exposure** – Companies may buy data to build databases to help reduce their risk. For example, a bank may build a database to better understand the types of individuals who may default on a loan.
3. **Data analytics** – Companies may buy personal data to help them understand the wants and needs of customers so they can better develop their products and services.

In this chapter, we are going to look at the circumstances in which this is allowed, along with the controls you must put in place to reduce the risk around buying personal data.

Complying with the data protection principles when buying personal data

Remember that there are 7 Data Protection Principles, which we discussed in Chapter 1. These are the seven commandments of GDPR and you must ensure that all of your data processing is consistent with these Data Protection Principles at all times.

As far as purchasing data from a third party goes, you must satisfy yourself that the purchase is consistent with the principles. For example:

- **Lawfulness, fairness and transparency**[125] – If you buy data, you should tell the data subjects about this in your Privacy Notices. (See Privacy Policy paragraph below).
- **Purpose limitation**[126] – Check that the seller is allowed to sell the personal data from you. For example, the seller cannot collect data for the purposes of customer administration and then go behind the customer's back and sell the data without the customer's knowledge.
- **Accuracy**[127] – If you do buy data, then you should check that it is accurate and up to date.

Performing Due Diligence on the data seller

GDPR is a tough regulation. It asks you to remain compliant with its multiple rules, but it also stipulates that you must be able to "demonstrate compliance" with the rules. Accountability is one of the key principles under GDPR. It demands that you are able to retain evidence of your compliance with all of the GDPR rules.[128]

If you are buying personal data, you should therefore conduct due diligence on the seller to make sure the data is legit. You should also keep records of that due diligence.

What specific questions should we ask the data seller before performing Due Diligence on them?

The ICO in its Direct Marketing Guidance[129] has set out some questions that may be appropriate to ask a third-party company before buying a marketing list. You may also find these Due Diligence questions useful if

[125] GDPR – Article 5(1)(a)

[126] GDPR – Article 5(1)(b)

[127] GDPR – Article 5(1)(d)

[128] GDPR – Article 5(2))

[129] ICO – Direct Marketing Guidance – June 2018 – Page 52

you are buying the personal data for non-marketing reasons, such as data analytics.

The ICO says:

"Reasonable due diligence might include checking the following:

Who compiled the list? When? Has it been amended or updated since then?

- *When was consent obtained?*
- *Who obtained it and in what context?*
- *What method was used – eg was it opt-in or opt-out?*
- *Was the information provided clear and intelligible? How was it provided – eg behind a link, in a footnote, in a pop-up box, in a clear statement next to the opt-in box?*
- *Did it specifically mention texts, emails or automated calls?*
- *Did it list organisations by name, by description, or was the consent for disclosure to any third party?*
- *Has the list been screened against the TPS or other relevant*
- *preference services? If so, when?*
- *Has the individual expressed any other preferences – eg regarding marketing calls or mail?*
- *Has the seller received any complaints?*
- *Is the seller a member of a professional body or accredited in some way?*

You might want to ask further questions relating to the Data Protection Principles including:

- *Did the data subjects know the third party would be selling the personal data?*
- *Is selling the personal data consistent with the original purpose for which the third party collected the personal data?*
- *Is the data being sold accurate and up to date?*

If the company cannot give you good answers to these questions, then you are taking a risk in buying the data from them.

What else should I ask the data seller for when I am doing my Due Diligence?

Do not take the data seller's word for anything. Ask them for relevant documents to support the answers they have given to your Due Diligence questions such as:

- **Consents** – Copies of the consents obtained from the data subjects.
- **Privacy Notices** – Copies of the consents the seller gave to the data subjects.
- **Accreditations** – Copies of accreditations that the seller has.
- **ICO Registration** – Details of the seller's registration with the ICO.
- **Policies** – Copies of the seller's Staff Data Protection Policy.

Performing a Data Protection Impact Assessment (DPIA)

It is recommended that you perform a Data Protection Impact Assessment (DPIA) before you buy any personal data from the data seller, to make sure any risks relating to the data purchase are mitigated.

See Chapter 3 for more details on DPIAs.

Contracts

It is important to put a contract in place with the data seller before any purchase takes place, in order to set out the rules of the game in terms of the personal data you are buying.

The ICO have said *"It would be prudent for a buyer to have a written contract in place confirming the reliability of the list, as well as making its own checks. The contract should give a buyer reasonable control and audit powers.*"[130]

The contracts should have indemnities in place to compensate you in the event that you incur loss or damage as a result of the seller providing substandard data or non-compliant data to your company.

Having a contract helps you to mitigate the risk around purchasing customer personal data. However, a contract is not a panacea.

Often, data sellers are very keen to sell their data for a high price and they say that a contract solves all problems. It does not. A contract cannot get you off the hook with a regulator if you have breached GDPR nor can it cover you against any GDPR fines issued by the ICO or any other EU Regulator. The contract is one part of the risk mitigation in relation to purchasing personal data, but it should not ever be the only control you put in place.

Privacy Notices

If you do decide to go ahead with a purchase of personal data, then you will need to ensure you provide the data subjects with privacy information about your company and the data processing you are carrying out.

You must take "appropriate measures" to make the Privacy Notice "easily accessible"[131]. This information must be provided to the data subjects "*within a reasonable period after obtaining the personal data but at the latest within one month*".[132]

Under Article 14 of GDPR, there are rules around giving privacy information to data subjects if you have obtained the personal data from a third party, such as a data seller.

130 ICO – Direct Marketing Guidance – Page 53 – 2018 – Soon to be updated

131 GDPR – Article 12

132 GDPR – Article 14(3)

Check that your Privacy Notice contains these details if you are going to purchase personal data.

See Chapter 13 for more details on Privacy Policies.

Buying Marketing Data

Does the company selling the data need the consent of the individuals to do so?

The company selling the personal data needs a lawful basis to sell the personal data under Article 6 of GDPR. Consent or legitimate interest are the likely bases upon which the data seller will be seeking to rely. Consent is often more reliable as it is easier to record and demonstrate.

If they are relying on legitimate interest, then they will have to be able to show that it was within the reasonable expectation of the individuals that their data would be sold in the way they propose doing. To rely on legitimate interest, the data seller must be able to show that they told the data subjects in their Privacy Notices or their correspondence with them that they would sell the data and they gave the individuals the opportunity to opt out of this (such as by saying if you do not wish to be involved in this, then please email us at Data.Protection@acme.com).

If the data seller does not have a lawful basis to sell the personal data, then they could get you in trouble after you buy it. It is up to your company to make sure you have asked the data seller for evidence of the legal basis on which you intend to rely.

Consent is needed to send emails, texts and for automated calls

You must be very careful if you are using a bought in list, to send marketing texts, emails or automated calls.[133]

For consumer marketing, you will need consent to send the individuals marketing texts, emails or automated calls.[134] In other words, you will

---

[133] ICO Guidance – Direct Marketing – 3 June 2018 – page 52

[134] PECR – Regulation 22

need evidence that the data subject has consented to your company buying their data and then sending marketing emails to the customer. The ICO says *"A buyer will only be able to send marketing texts or emails, or make automated calls, to people on the list if they gave specific consent. In most cases, indirect consent- that is, consent given to someone other than the organisation doing the marketing – will not be enough for this"*. They also say *"a list with general consent to third party marketing may be enough for mail marketing, but is unlikely to cover calls, texts or emails".*[135] *They go on to say "If you are buying a 'consented' marketing list, the consent request must have identified you specifically."*[136]

You should ask the data seller for evidence of their consent before relying on it.

The ICO says *"A reputable list broker should be able to demonstrate that the marketing list for sale or rental is reliable.....If the seller cannot provide this information, a buyer should not use the list"*.[137]

For example:

- Red List Brokers wants to sell its personal data marketing list to Blue Insurance.
- Blue Insurance buy the list from Red List Brokers.
- The list contains 50 customer names.
- Blue Insurance wants to send these customers marketing emails about their insurance products and services.
- Blue Insurance should check to ensure that the data subjects gave consent to Red List Brokers.

---

[135] ICO Guidance – Direct Marketing – 3 June 2018 page 50

[136] ICO Guidance – Direct Marketing – 3 June 2018 page 51

[137] ICO Guidance – Direct Marketing – 3 June 2018 page 53

- For Blue Insurance to be able to rely on the consent, they need to make sure that the data subjects agreed to receive marketing material from Blue Insurance.
- Blue Insurance ask Red List Brokers for evidence of the consents that the data subjects provided to Red List Brokers that mention Blue Insurance.
- They must analyse these consents to make sure they are good enough before relying on them.

See Chapter 4 for more details on the Marketing Rules.

For business to business marketing

If you buy any personal data for business to business marketing (such as personal corporate email addresses, such as Dave.Jones@BigCorporation.com) then you should make sure you have:

Either:

a. Consent that allows your company to send marketing to the business contact (such as Dave.Jones@BigCorporation.com), OR

b. A legitimate interest to contact the business contact.

If you do intend to market to the business contact, then you must give them the opportunity to opt out of receiving further communications.

See Chapter 4 for more details on the Marketing Rules.

Recap and Practical steps to take:

1. **Data Protection Impact Assessment** – Perform a DPIA on any incidences of data selling before they take place.
2. **Due Diligence** – Perform Due Diligence on all data sellers before buying personal data from them.
3. **Marketing** – Be very careful when buying personal data in order to use it for marketing purposes. Consent is needed to send

ordinary customers marketing texts or emails under the PECR. If you are relying on consent obtained from the data seller, you must ask to see evidence of those consents.

4. **Contracts** – Ensure there is a contract in place between your company and the data seller.

5. **Privacy Notices** – Ensure your Privacy Notices give sufficient information to data subjects, if you have bought data relating to them.

CHAPTER EIGHT

ARTIFICIAL INTELLIGENCE (AI) IN FINANCIAL SERVICES

What is Artificial Intelligence?

The financial services sector is being revolutionised by Artificial Intelligence ('AI'). The ICO has defined AI as '*the theory and development of computer systems able to perform tasks normally requiring human intelligence*' in their ICO Guidance on AI and Data Protection.[138]

In movies such as 'Terminator 2' and Steven Spielberg's 'AI', Artificial Intelligence was science fiction. AI is now a big part of our reality. Financial services companies are harnessing the great power of AI.

AI is a vast subject with a huge number of legal and data protection implications. This chapter cannot discuss them all. Rather, this chapter gives a brief summary of some of the main AI issues as they relate to GDPR.

Why is AI important in financial services?

Financial services companies use data across their operations and central functions for numerous different reasons.

They may use AI for a number of reasons.

Below are a few brief examples:

- **Fraud Prevention** – AI can help companies avoid fraud. For example, AI may be used to detect insurance fraud or money laundering through monitoring customer interactions and activity.

---

[138] ICO Guidance on AI and Data Protection – July 2020 – Page 8

- **Process automation** – AI can help firms automate processes that you would normally expect humans to do. For example, Big Bank receives thousands of loan applications per year. They reject approximately 1,000 loan applications a year. In the old days, Big Bank used to send the names of the people who had been rejected to the administration department who then drafted up the loan rejection letters. Big Bank have now automated this process using AI. When a loan is rejected, a letter is automatically drafted by computer and sent out.

- **Compliance** – AI can help companies with their compliance obligations. For example, AI can be used to conduct sanctions screening checks or Know Your Customer (KYC) Checks.

- **Credit checking** – AI can help banks and other financial institutions to check on a person's credit quickly and easily.

- **Customer service** – AI can help companies automate their customer service. For example, Chatbots (a software application used to have online chats with customers) and other forms of software such as voice recognition can provide individualised customer service quickly and efficiently.

- **Marketing** – AI can help companies in financial services to send customers marketing that is more efficient. For example, AI can help align customer preferences with the advertising they receive.

Regulators, Artificial Intelligence and a risk-based approach

As AI becomes more prevalent within companies, the authorities are starting to pay closer attention to the subject.

In April 2021, the European Commission published a new draft regulation governing the use of AI.

The Financial Conduct Authority in the UK has said "*Data analytics and AI are increasingly used in financial markets. ...... Where decisions are taken by financial services firms using data-based or algorithmic methods, we need to make sure those decisions are transparent, fair and secure, and that the data is used ethically."*

In July 2020, the ICO has released very comprehensive guidance on the subject called 'Guidance on AI and Data Protection'. The ICO has said that organisations should adopt a risk-based approach when processing personal data for the purposes of Artificial Intelligence.

In particular, they say:

"Taking a risk-based approach means:

- *assessing the risks to the rights and freedoms of individuals that may arise when you use AI;*
- *implementing appropriate and proportionate technical and organisational measures to mitigate these risks."*[139]

Legal issues to consider in respect of AI

Data Protection Principles

As we discussed in Chapter 1, the Data Protection Principles must be observed by your company when using AI.

The Principles are:

1. Lawfulness, fairness and transparency

This is important in the context of AI. In particular, you must:

- Be up front with your customers about how their personal data is processed and tell them about this in your Privacy Notices.
- Ensure the AI does not lead to unfair outcomes, such as inadvertently discriminating against the customer.

[139] ICO Guidance on AI and Data Protection – July 2020 – Page 8

2. Purpose limitation

You cannot collect personal data for one purpose and go behind the customer's back to use it for a different purpose, such as AI, if the AI is incompatible with the first purpose.

3. Data minimisation

Personal data shall be adequate, relevant and limited to what is necessary in relation to the purposes for which they are processed. Don't let AI applications process too much irrelevant data.

4. Accuracy

Personal data must be accurate and, where necessary, kept up to date. You must ensure the data you are using for the AI is accurate so that the AI does not lead to unfair outcomes.

For example, Shady Insurers use AI to help them decide what insurance price quotes they should give to various customers. Jim contacts Shady to get a car insurance quote. Shady has out of date data on Jim, including details relating to a speeding ticket he received 20 years ago. Shady use this data to provide a quote to Jim via their AI system. As a result of using this old, out of date personal data, Jim is given a quote for his car insurance that is too high and unfair to him.

5. Storage limitation

Don't retain the personal data you process in your AI projects for longer than is necessary.

6. Security

Make sure there is appropriate security around the data you use for AI.

7. Accountability

Keep records of the controls you have in place around AI in case you are ever asked for copies of these records by a Regulator.

For example, you should keep records of any Data Protection Impact Assessments you approved for the use of AI.

Legal basis under Article 6

As we have discussed in Chapter 1, any time personal data is processed, there must be a legal basis in place under GDPR to process the personal data.

The legal bases appear at Article 6 of GDPR and those most relevant to AI are set out below. The ICO says "*whenever you are processing personal data – whether to train a new AI system, or make predictions using an existing one – you must have an appropriate lawful basis to do so.*"[140]

The Legal bases perhaps most relevant to AI processing are potentially the bases set out below. We discuss these briefly.

a) **Consent of the data subject** [141]- The data subject has given consent to the processing of his or her personal data through the use of AI. The benefit of using consent as a lawful basis is that valid consent can be easier to document and show to a regulator in the event that you are questioned about your lawful basis in relation to the AI. The disadvantage is that the consent can be withdrawn by the individual.

b) **Contractual necessity**[142] – Processing is necessary for the performance of a contract to which the data subject is party or in order to take steps at the request of the data subject prior to entering into a contract. In other words, if you need the AI to deliver a contractual service to the individual, then this may be appropriate. For example, in some cases, some insurers may (depending on the circumstances) be able to rely on this ground for the purposes of using AI to assess the policyholder's circumstances in order to price their insurance policy.

c) **Legal obligation**[143] – Processing is necessary for compliance with a legal obligation to which the controller is subject. Is there any law that obliges you to perform AI on a customer's data? For example, for anti-

---

[140] ICO Guidance on AI and Data Protection – July 2020 – Page 29

[141] GDPR – Article 6(1)(a)

[142] GDPR – Article 6(1)(b)

[143] GDPR – Article 6(1)(c)

money laundering purposes or something of that nature. Remember, it must be a legal obligation, not a legal discretion.

d) **Legitimate interest of your firm**[144] – Processing is necessary for the purposes of the legitimate interests pursued by the Controller or by a third party, except where such interests are overridden by the interests or fundamental rights and freedoms of the data subject. This is the vaguest and most contentious legal basis. Your company may be able to rely on this ground for AI processing if you can:

- Identify a legitimate interest (the 'purpose test');
- Show that the processing is necessary to achieve it (the 'necessity test'); and
- Balance it against the individual's interests, rights and freedoms (the 'balancing test').[145]

The Article 9 Legal Basis – Special Category Personal Data

If your firm is processing special category data, such as personal data relating to race, politics, religion, genetics, biometrics, health, sex life or sexuality, whilst using AI, then you will need one of the legal bases we have set out above. You will also need a further legal basis under Article 9 of GDPR such as:

- Explicit Consent, or
- Substantial Public Interest

See Chapter 1 for more details.

---

[144] GDPR – Article 6(1)(f)

[145] ICO Guidance on AI and Data Protection – July 2020 – Page 33

Processors and Controllers

Often data processing using AI involves multiple stakeholders. For example, you might purchase an AI application from a third-party provider. Alternatively, you might work with another financial institution to set up a fraud database for your mutual benefit that uses AI.

When you are working with other parties and processing personal data that uses AI, it is important to determine who the Processors are and who the Controllers are in respect of the personal data.

A Controller is 'the natural or legal person, public authority or other body which, alone or jointly with others determines the purposes and means of the processing of personal data'.

In other words, they decide how and why the person's personal data is processed.

'Processor' means a natural or legal person, public authority, agency or other body which processes personal data on behalf of the Controller.

You may need to put contractual clauses in place to govern the relationship between you and any third parties with whom you are engaged in processing personal data that uses AI. See Chapter 10.

Profiling and Automated Decision making

The Right to have human oversight in a decision made by a computer

Article 22 of GDPR says:

"The data subject shall have the right not to be subject to a decision based solely on automated processing, including profiling, which produces legal effects concerning him or her or similarly significantly affects him or her."

In other words, people have a right to have human oversight in a decision that has been made by a computer, [146] such as when an AI application refuses a loan to a bank customer.

[146] GDPR – Article 22(1)

If you do have any AI applications that process personal data by computer and make decisions that significantly affect people, then you must make changes to your processes. You must ensure individuals who have their data processed using AI can:

- Obtain human oversight or intervention in the decision, and
- Express their point of view, and
- Receive an explanation of the decision and challenge it.

For example:

- Riley sees her dream home for sale in Cookstown.
- She decides to make an offer and the offer is accepted. Riley sees an online application for a mortgage with Dream Mortgages.
- She enters her details. Dream Mortgages use an AI application to process Riley's personal data.
- Three weeks later, she receives an email telling her that her mortgage application has been refused.
- When Riley asks Dream about this, they tell her that a computer reviews the applications. Riley is now in danger of missing out on the sale.
- Dream must make sure that one of their employees can review the mortgage applications that the AI software has refused.

There are some exceptions to the rule that companies must have a human review of computer decisions, including if:

- The processing is necessary for a contract between the data subject and the Controller, or
- The data subject has consented to the processing.[147]

[147] GDPR – Article 22(2)

Mitigating your risks in relation to AI – Practical Steps to Take

As the ICO has said, you must mitigate your data protection risks in relation to the personal data processing you are doing for AI purposes.

Some of the steps you can take to mitigate any data protection risk related to the use of AI appear below.

1. Updating your Privacy Notices to tell people about how their data is processed using AI systems

We include more information on your Privacy Notice obligations at Chapter 12. In your Privacy Notice, you should tell individuals if you process any of their personal data using AI. Give details on your Privacy Policy about any computer decision-making you are doing in relation to the AI you use.

2. Data Protection Impact Assessments (DPIAs)

It is advisable to do a DPIA on any processing of personal data that uses AI.

The ICO has said *"in the majority of cases, you are legally required to complete a DPIA if you use AI systems that process personal data. DPIAs offer you an opportunity to consider how and why you are using AI systems to process personal data and what the potential risks should be*[148]*".*

For more details on DPIAs, see Chapter 3.

3. Contracts

If you are engaging with multiple stakeholders in relation to processing personal data using AI, then you should ensure you have contracts in place with these various stakeholders.

148 ICO Guidance on AI and Data Protection – July 2020 – Page 4

For example, if you use an outsourced AI provider who is a Processor and they are processing personal data on your behalf, then you need a contract in place with the provider that includes all of the processor clauses set out in Article 28 of GDPR.

If you are processing personal data using AI with another Controller, then it is a good idea to put a contract in place setting out what your various responsibilities are in respect of the personal data.

4. Anonymisation

Sometimes, you may be able to derive value from processing data using AI, even if the personal data is fully anonymised. Anonymised data is *"information which does not relate to an identified or identifiable natural person or to personal data rendered anonymous in such a manner that the data subject is not or no longer identifiable."*[149] Anonymised data is outside the scope of GDPR.

If you can achieve the same aims on the AI project with anonymised data, then you should anonymise the data.

[149] GDPR – Recital 26

CHAPTER NINE

DATA SECURITY AND REPORTING DATA BREACHES

Introduction

Security is the most important part of GDPR compliance. Keeping personal data safe is the most important rule of privacy and data protection.

The largest GDPR fines in the UK have been levied against companies for breaches of security. The ICO fined a hotel company £18.4 million for failing to keep millions of customers' personal data secure following a cyber-attack.[150] The ICO fined an airline £20 million following a cyber-attack for failing to protect the personal and financial details of more than 400,000 of its customers.[151]

Data security impacts companies in financial services for a number of reasons including:

- The sheer amount of data they hold
- The sensitivity of some of that data
- The fact that financial services companies are often the target of cyber attackers

Improving your company's data security should be your number one priority under GDPR.

150 https://ico.org.uk/about-the-ico/news-and-events/news-and-blogs/2020/10/ico-fines-marriott-international-inc-184million-for-failing-to-keep-customers-personal-data-secure/.

151 https://ico.org.uk/about-the-ico/news-and-events/news-and-blogs/2020/10/ico-fines-british-airways-20m-for-data-breach-affecting-more-than-400-000-customers/.

What does the GDPR expect on Data Security?

The principle of data security is one of the key Data Protection Principles.

Article 5 of GDPR says:

Personal data shall be processed in a manner that:

- *ensures appropriate security of the personal data*
- *including protection against unauthorised or unlawful processing*
- *and against accidental loss, destruction or damage*
- *using appropriate technical or organisational measures.*[152]

The security principle is one of the 7 Data Protection Principles.

What else does GDPR say on security?

Article 32 of GDPR says:

"The controller and the processor shall implement appropriate technical and organisational measures to ensure a level of security appropriate to the risk".

In other words, your company should take steps to keep data secure based on the risk posed by the personal data being lost. The greater the risk posed by data being lost, the more you have to ensure that the steps you have taken are sufficient to keep the data secure.

Article 32 says that you should take into account a number of factors when deciding on the types of security measures you put in place:

"The state of the art, the costs of implementation and the nature, scope, context and purposes of processing as well as the risk of varying likelihood and severity for the rights and freedoms of natural persons".

They also say that your security should include, where appropriate:

a) **Using pseudonymisation** (e.g. taking out the identifiers from your data and storing them separately to increase security)

[152] GDPR – Article 5(1)(f)

b) **Encryption**

c) **Keeping your systems secure**

d) **Being able to restore your systems after an incident**

e) **Regularly testing your systems to ensure they are secure**

As we can see, GDPR says that it is up to you to make a judgment on the type of security you need, taking into account the risk posed to individuals by that data being lost or compromised.

Does GDPR mandate encryption?

GDPR says you should use encryption where it is appropriate to do so. [153]Encryption is a very important part of Data Protection and you should use it as much as possible to keep your data safe.

For example, strong encryption controls should definitely be in place with higher risk types of data such as credit card information. If you do suffer a data breach and the data is properly encrypted, then you may not have to report the incident to individuals. Encryption can protect your company against reputational damage and litigation in the event of a data breach.[154]

Security – The perpetual campaign

Security is an ongoing requirement. No company can install security controls in their company and claim to be forever compliant on data security. Data security is a perpetual campaign. Systems and controls must constantly be monitored and updated to ensure data remains secure. GDPR says there should be "ongoing" security[155]along with "regular testing".[156]

---

153 GDPR – Article 32(1((a)

154 GDPR – Article 34(3)(a)

155 GDPR – Article 32(1)(b)

156 GDPR – Article 32(1)(d)

Security priorities

GDPR expects you to take a risk-based approach to security. You should consider the *"risk.... and severity for the rights and freedoms of natural persons"*.

All personal data is not created equal. There is personal data that could cause more loss and damage to individuals (and to your company) in the event of a data breach. It is advisable to have added security over the riskier data elements first.

For example:

- Julie is the Data Protection Officer for Platinum Bank.
- Platinum hold credit card data relating to thousands of customers on a database called 'DB 1'.
- The security controls in place around this database are not adequate as there is insufficient encryption in place.
- Whilst Julie has a number of concerns about personal data security across the company, she decides to make 'DB 1' her priority due to the quantity and sensitivity of the personal data involved.
- She acts today to safeguard this data.

Practical steps you can take in implementing security

Security is a vast and very dynamic area. There is not a one-size-fits-all recommendation on the security controls that should be in place. Below, we set out some of the potential security controls you may wish to consider. This is not a complete list and there will be many further controls that could benefit your company. Your IT Security Team can help you understand what the best security controls for your company are.

Twelve suggested security controls:

1. **Encryption** – As discussed, encryption is a very important security control. Having strong encryption controls in place reduces your regulatory risk in the event that personal data is ever lost or compromised. Putting a good Encryption Policy in place in your company will help ensure sensible encryption controls are implemented.

2. **Pseudonymisation** – Pseudonymisation is a good tool. It involves taking out identifiers in personal data sets in order to limit the risk around the personal data processing.

   For example, First Insurance in the UK want to send a table containing some personal data relating to 500 employees to an external payroll provider called Payz. The personal data relating to their employees includes salary details and details of absences due to illness. To reduce the risk in sending this personal data, First Insurance take out the names of the individuals and replace each employee name with a number. They then send the table to Payz.

3. **Anonymisation** – Do you need to use personal data for the project you are working on? If you are able to anonymise the personal data, then you should do so. "In order to be truly anonymised under the UK GDPR, you must strip personal data of sufficient elements that mean the individual can no longer be identified."[157]

4. **Policies** – GDPR says you must "implement the appropriate data protection policies". [158]These policies should include your Data Protection Policy and Information Security Policy. If staff members breach these policies, they should be disciplined.

5. **Staff training** – Staff mistakes are the single biggest cause of data breaches. One study stated that human error caused 90% of cyber data breaches in 2019, according to an analysis of data from the

[157] ICO – What is personal data? –. https://ico.org.uk/.

[158] GDPR – Article 24(2)

ICO.[159] Take steps to ensure your employees know their responsibilities on Data Protection by giving them training, at least annually.

Training topics may include:

- Your company's Data Protection Policy
- How to avoid falling victim to phishing attempts and other frauds
- Keeping desks clear
- Locking screens
- Respecting building security
- Maintaining good passwords

6. **Access controls** – Only those individuals who need to have access to personal data should have access to it. You must ensure your systems are configured in such a way that only those individuals who should be able to see data can actually access it in practice. [160] You need to be careful to ensure that contractors and former employees have their access controls to your offices and systems immediately removed after they leave your company.

7. **Technology** – GDPR expects you to put appropriate technology in place to ensure your data security is up to par. Your company should ensure you have appropriate technology in place to ensure your personal data is kept sufficiently secure. Examples of technology you may wish to consider includes:

   - Antivirus software

---

[159] www.infosecurity-magazine.com. 90% of UK Data Breaches Due to Human Error in 2019 – 6 February 2020

[160] GDPR – Article 5(1)(c)

- Malware protection software
- Email security software
- Incident detection software
- Data Loss Prevention (DLP) software
- Multi-factor authentication

8. **Physical security** – This area includes ensuring that your building is sufficiently secure so that interlopers are not able to try to access your systems. Having appropriate entry controls is important, as is having appropriate CCTV in place.

9. **Pen Testing** – Penetration Testing is where authorised individuals, such as your IT Security Department or authorised IT service providers, try to hack into your network in order to test the robustness of your security controls. It is a vital part of any data security program. Your IT Security Team should ensure that you commit to a regular program.

10. **Incident response** – Your company should have a Data Breach Incident Response Policy and procedure in place so that your company knows how to:
    - Recognise a Data Breach when it happens
    - Contain a Data Breach to stop more data from being lost
    - Learn lessons from previous data breaches so they do not reoccur

We deal with incident responses to data breaches in more detail towards the end of this chapter.

11. **Previous security investigations and audits at your company**
    It is advisable to try and understand whether there have been any previous audits in relation to your security controls. These audits may have been conducted by:

- Your Internal Audit Team
- External auditors you may have hired to assess your security controls
- Your IT Security Team
- Your Data Protection Officer

It is advisable to read these reports to understand:

- What the recommendations were to improve security
- Whether the recommendations were implemented
- What you should do in order to prioritise security at your company

12. **Cyber insurance** – It is advisable to ensure you have the appropriate level of cyber insurance in place to cover you against data breaches or cyber-attacks. You should check the level of cover you have in place and upgrade your policy, if necessary.

Third parties

A vital part of ensuring security includes dealing with third party providers and business partners to whom you entrust your personal data. This includes:

- Performing appropriate due diligence on third parties before you contract with them.
- Putting contracts in place to ensure third parties safeguard personal data processed on your behalf.

See Chapter 10 for more details on dealing with third parties.

Assessing your own security

Assessing your own data security can be a complicated and, at times, daunting task. However, *"a Journey of a Thousand Miles Begins with a Single Step."*

It is recommended that you firstly draw up a plan to assess your own security controls. Over the longer term, you can act to fill these gaps but in the immediate term, you should try and gain a high-level of understanding of your main security concerns.

For example, Katherine is Gem Asset Manager's Data Protection Officer. Katherine decides to audit Gem's data security controls. She engages stakeholders across the business including IT Security, Building Security, HR, Compliance and Legal. Katherine asks them a number of questions about security controls relevant to their area. When she receives the answers, she thinks about some of the next steps she could take. She sets it out in the table below:

Data Security Issue	Questions	Answers	Next steps
Technology	Have we appropriate technology in place, such as: • Antivirus software • Malware protection software • Email security software • Incident detection software • Data Loss Prevention (DLP) software • Multi-factor authentication •	Answers include the following: • Software in place in some instances. • Software is out of date in many instances and has not been updated. • Complaints from Breach Response Team that software has not been update.	Next steps: • Investigate whether the software can be updated. • Speak to IT Team and ascertain their views on the software.

Employees	• Do employees receive any training on data security? • Do employees know how to report a data breach to the DPO? • What access do employees have to customer data?	• No annual Data Protection Training.	Train employees on: • Your company's Data Protection Policy • How to avoid falling victim to phishing attempts and other frauds • Keeping desks clear • Locking screens • Respecting building security • Maintaining good passwords
Policies and Procedures	• Do you have adequate policies and procedures in place?	• Policies on Data Protection and IT Security seem out of date. • No Encryption Policy in place.	• Update Data Protection and IT Security policies. • Draft Encryption Policy.
Third parties	• Which third parties have access to our data? • Are there contracts in place to ensure that third parties behave when they are handling our data?	• Legal do not have a record of the third party with whom we share personal data. • There are some contracts but some of them do not have the Article 28 GDPR clauses.	• Maintain record of all third parties processing personal data on our behalf. • Update contracts to include GDPR clauses.

Incident response	• Is there an incident response Team and Policy? • Are they able to properly detect incidents and data breaches as they occur?	• Team in place that is undertrained. • No clear policy. • Difficulty in detecting breaches as they occur as there is inadequate data incident response software in place.	• Speak to IT Security about obtaining Data Breach response software. • Train the Incident Response Team on their responsibilities. • Put clear Incident response Policy and plan in place.
Building Security	• Is the building secure? • Are the entrance controls sufficient?	• Reception unmanned. • Building security lax. • No CCTV.	• Speak with Building Security about putting improvements in place.

Breach notification

Under GDPR, there are responsibilities to report certain data breaches to individuals, regulators and Data Controllers (if you are a Data Processor).

We set out these responsibilities below.

What is a personal data breach under GDPR?

A personal data breach means 'a breach of security leading to the accidental or unlawful destruction, loss, alteration, unauthorised disclosure of, or access to, personal data transmitted, stored or otherwise processed.'[161]

[161] GDPR – Article 4(12)

When must you report data breaches to the EU Supervisory Authorities/the UK ICO if you are a Controller?

If there is a risk to individuals – If you are a Controller, you must report data breaches to Regulators under GDPR if the breach is likely to result in a risk to the rights and freedoms of natural persons.

Within 72 hours – The Controller must report the breach to the Regulator within 72 hours of becoming aware of the data breach.

This obligation appears at Article 33(1) of GDPR.

When must you report data breaches to the Controller if you are a Processor?

Processors must tell the Controller about all data breaches involving personal data they are processing on behalf of the Controller. If a data breach happens on the Processor's watch, then they must tell their Controller.

All data breaches – If you are a Processor, you must report all data breaches to the Controller.

Without undue delay – The Processor must notify the Controller without undue delay.

This obligation appears at Article 33(2) of GDPR.

When must you report data breaches to individual data subjects when you are a Controller?

If there is a <u>high</u> risk to individuals – If you are a Controller, you must report data breaches to individuals under GDPR if the breach is likely to result in a <u>high</u> risk to the rights and freedoms of natural persons.

Without undue delay – The Controller must communicate the data breach to the data subjects without undue delay.[162]

---

[162] GDPR – Article 34(1)

Encryption – If you have used encryption or any other means that would make the personal data unintelligible to the unauthorised person, then you do not have to report the data breach to the individuals.[163]

Public communication – You can only inform the data subjects by public communication such as a website notice (as opposed to a direct communication, such as an email) if it would involve a disproportionate effort to send each data subject a direct communication.[164]

If you do have to report a data breach to a Regulator (such as the ICO in the UK), then what do you have to include in your breach report?

The notification referred to the regulator shall include details of:

- **The nature of the breach** – The nature of the personal data breach, including where possible, the categories and approximate number of data subjects concerned and the categories and approximate number of personal data records concerned.

- **Your DPO** – Communicate the name and contact details of the Data Protection Officer.

- **The consequences** – The likely consequences of the personal data breach.

- **The risk mitigations taken** – Describe the measures taken or proposed to be taken by the Controller to address the personal data breach.

- **Phases** – Where you cannot provide all the information at once, you can do so in phases, as long as you do not delay in doing so.[165]

---

163 GDPR – Article 34(3)(a)

164 GDPR – Article 34(3)(c)

165 GDPR – Article 33(4)

Records – GDPR says you must keep records of any personal data breaches, including the facts and any action you took to remedy the breach.[166]

If you do have to report a data breach to a data subject, then what details do you have to include in your communication?

The communication to the data subject shall include details of:

- **Your DPO** – Communicate the name and contact details of the Data Protection Officer.
- **The consequences** – The likely consequences of the personal data breach.
- **The risk mitigations taken** – Describe the measures taken or proposed to be taken by the Controller to address the personal data breach.[167]

Practical steps to take in relation to reporting data breaches

1. **Template letters** – It is wise to put template communications or letters in place so that you have them ready in case you ever do need to report a data breach.

   It is advisable to put a template letter in place for:

   - **Data subjects** -The template letter should explain the likely consequences of the breach, the details of your DPO and any risk mitigations in place.
   - **Regulators** – The template letter should explain the nature of the breach including the number of records, the likely consequences of the breach, the details of your DPO and any risk mitigations in place. Many GDPR regulators, such

[166] GDPR – Article 33(5)

[167] GDPR – Article 34(2)

as the ICO, only accept breach reports via their online portal but having a template in place will help you draft up the report you make via the portal.

- **Processors reporting breaches to your Controllers** – If you act as a Processor, you should have a template similar to the above in place to allow you to report breaches to your Controller client. Financial Services Companies are more often Controllers.

2. **Data Breach Response Policy** – Your company should put a Data Breach Response Policy in place setting out your company policy on:

   - How incidents are detected, investigated and reported.
   - Which stakeholders are responsible for each of the above steps.
   - How communications to Regulators and consumers should be approved by your compliance and Legal Departments.

3. **Training** – Ensure your breach response team have the appropriate training on how to handle data breach incidents. Make sure you have rehearsed the plan so that everyone knows what to do in the event that a real data breach incident occurs.

4. **Incident detection software** – A former director of the FBI once said ""*There are only two types of companies: Those that have been hacked and those that will be hacked."* A big part of breach management is to have the appropriate technology in place to alert you to a data breach incident that has happened at your company. Work with your IT Security Team to ensure that you have the best possible incident detection software.

CHAPTER TEN

SHARING DATA WITH THIRD PARTIES

Third parties and financial services

Sharing personal data with third party companies is an absolute necessity in financial services. This sharing can be potentially risky. Often, when you hear about data breach incidents in the news, it involves a company losing data due to the actions of a third-party supplier. One of the most important parts of Data Protection involves managing third party risk.

Some of the biggest data breaches in history have involved third parties dropping the ball.

In one famous breach back in 2013, an American retail corporation was hacked. The hackers gained access to the corporation's data. They did so by hacking into the systems of one of the corporation's air conditioning suppliers. The hackers gained access of up to 40 million people's credit cards. The breach was estimated to have cost the company $202 million.[168]

A company in the financial services sector may share personal data with hundreds, or even thousands of third-party businesses.

For example, an insurance company may share personal data with a range of external companies including:

- Third party insurance companies
- Companies managing anti-fraud databases
- Underwriters
- External lawyers

---

[168] NBC News – Target settles 2013 Hacked Customer Data Breach

- Payroll providers
- IT service providers
- Cloud providers
- Marketing companies
- Document shredding companies
- Data analytics companies

In this chapter, we are going to look at the circumstances in which we share personal data externally. We will look at the controls we must put in place to manage these risks.

Managing the risks

The external companies with whom your company shares personal data fall into two main categories:

a) **Suppliers** – Companies providing a service for you and processing personal data on your behalf and acting on your instructions. Sometimes, suppliers are referred to as 'vendors'.

b) **Business partners** – Companies working on projects with you that are not acting solely on your instructions.

In order to manage the risks relating to this data sharing, you must put contracts in place that govern how personal data must be handled.

The contracts required will differ depending on whether the third-party company with whom you share the data is a Controller or a Processor.

Controllers, Processors, Joint Controller and Sub-Processors – A quick reminder

Every company that processes personal data is either a Processor or a Controller, depending on the level of autonomy it has in relation to the data. If the company processing the data is acting on instructions and merely doing what it is told with the data, then the company is likely to be a Processor. If it has more control or autonomy over the data, then it is likely to be a Controller.

A Controller is the company which 'determines the purposes and means of the processing of personal data'[169].

For example, Big Bank is a Controller for its customer and employee data.

A Processor is a company which 'processes personal data on behalf of the Controller.[170]

For example, Big Bank use Eezy Payroll to process their employee payroll data. Eezy is a Processor.

A Joint Controller is 'two or more controllers jointly determining the purposes and means of the processing'. [171]

For example, Big Bank shares data with Tiny Bank. They are both in charge of building a large database of customer marketing details that they will both own and operate together to help them in a mutual marketing venture. They are joint controller.

It is always helpful to come back to the definitions above when deciding whether a company is a Processor or a Controller.

A Sub-Processor is a company used by the Processor to help them with some of the data processing operations.

For example, Big Bank is a Controller and it uses Eezy Payroll to process the employee payroll data. Eezy is a Processor. Eeezy use a Sub-Processor cloud provider to help them store the personal data.

---

169 GDPR – Article 4(7) GDPR

170 GDPR – Article 4(8)

171 GDPR – Article 26(1)

Why is the Controller/Processor question so important?

The rules for contracts differ based on whether the contract is between:

- A Controller and a Processor or,
- A Controller and another Controller

There are also different rules in place on the type of contracts you need, depending on whether the party with whom you are sharing data is a Processor or a Controller. We will come to the contracts that are required when you share personal data with a Processor and when you share personal data with a Controller. Firstly, we must look at vetting the third parties with whom you share data, before you share the data with them.

Is my company always a Controller?

If your company is a financial services company, then it is going to be a Controller in respect of its own employee and customer data. Your company will share data with many third parties. Some of those third parties will be Controllers and some will be Processors, depending on the level of autonomy the third party has over the data processing.

I'm confused. I don't know whether the third-party company is a Controller or a Processor?

It isn't always easy to discern whether a third-party company is a Processor or a Controller. It always helps to look at the evidence when deciding whether a company is a Processor. For example, look at:

- Any contracts that are already in existence with the third party. Do the contract terms point towards the company being a Processor?
- The data processing that the third party is doing. Are they acting only on your instructions to help you or are they processing the personal data for their own reasons?

Remember, the contracts you have to draft differ depending on whether the third party is a Processor or a Controller, so it is important that you get this question right.

Part A – How to mitigate risk when your company is a Controller and is sharing personal data with a Processor.

Vetting the Processor

Your financial services company will hire many third-party companies to help it with its operations including cloud providers, payroll providers and document shredders. If the third-party company has no autonomy over the data that you provide to them, then they will be a Processor.

One of the main things you must do as a company is to keep your customer and employee data secure.

A big part of that security involves vetting the third parties with whom you share personal data, especially when you are hiring Processors to process personal data on your behalf.

Under GDPR 'the controller shall use only processors providing sufficient guarantees' that they will implement proper security.[172] [173] This means there is a responsibility on your company to do background checks on the Processor BEFORE you sign a contract with them. In other words, you must do 'Due Diligence' on the supplier.

What kind of Due Diligence is needed?

It makes sense to ask the Processor for information on:

a) Their Privacy Notices and Policies

b) Their Staff training on Privacy

---

[172] GDPR – Article 28(1)

[173] GDPR – Recital 81

c) Their data protection program including whether they have a Data Protection Officer

d) Details of the data security they would use to keep your data safe including encryption, firewalls, anti-virus etc

e) Details on where the data will be processed

f) Whether they have suffered any data breaches in the past

g) Whether they have been fined or received notices or complaints from Data Protection Regulators

h) Details of Data Protection Audits they have performed on their programme

i) Details in respect of the Sub-Processors they use

j) Whether they have any security certifications such as ISO 27001

k) What the details are of their registration with the ICO (if in the UK) or any other EU Regulators

Remember, you need "sufficient guarantees" from the Processor that they will keep your personal information secure. Do not hesitate to ask the Processor for proof that they will keep your data secure. For example, ask to see policies and procedures and don't take the Processor's word that they have the policies in place. GDPR is a "show not tell" regulation. We need proof of compliance and we need records of compliance in respect of our personal data processing because GDPR demands that we are able to "*demonstrate compliance*".[174]

You should put a Due Diligence Questionnaire in place that asks the Processor to provide evidence of their compliance, including the issues outlined at (a)-(k) above.

Signing the Processor up to a Contract.

The contract between the Controller and the Processor is known as a Data Processing Agreement or a 'DPA'. Sometimes, the DPA is in a

[174] GDPR – Article 5(2)

standalone contract and sometimes it is annexed to the main contract clauses.

What clauses must we put in the Processor contract?

The contract [175]must set out:

- **The subject matter and duration of the processing** – E.g. This is a 1year contract for cloud services.
- **The nature and purpose of the processing** – E.g. This is to host the data in order to ensure maximum security over the data.
- **The type of personal data involved** – E.g. Our customer contact details.
- **The categories of data subjects**[176] – E.g. Customers.

The contract must also include the clauses below:

a. **Does what they are told** – The Processor processes the personal data only on documented instructions from the Controller.[177]

b. **Manages their employees** – The employees must be told to keep the personal data confidential.[178]

c. **Has enough Security** – The Processor must have an appropriate level of security in place.[179] Security is an important part of the contract. Make sure to ask your Processor to set out the security you require. For example, you might ask them to use encryption, anonymisation, access controls, audit logs, data loss prevention monitoring and many other controls. See Chapter 9 for more details on Security measures.

---

[175] GDPR – Article 28

[176] GDPR – Article 28(3)

[177] GDPR – Article 28(3)(a)

[178] GDPR – Article 28(3)(b)

[179] GDPR – Article 28(3)(c)

d. **Can only hire their own Sub-Processors to help them if they have consent** – The Processor will only engage a Sub-Processor to help them process the personal data if they have your consent and the Sub-Processor is signed up to the same contractual terms that you have placed on the Processor.[180]

e. **Will help the Controller with GDPR customer requests** – The Processor has measures in place to help the Controller with any GDPR rights requests that the Controller receives from their own customers. For example, you may receive a request from your customer to access their data. However, the Processor may be holding that data on your behalf and you need them to provide you with a copy of the data so you can send it on to your customer.[181]

f. **Will report data breaches to the Controller** – The Processor will assist the Controller with their other obligations, such as reporting data breaches in good time.[182]

g. **Will delete the data at the end of the contracts** – The Processor deletes or returns all the personal data to the Controller after the end of the contract.[183]

h. **Audit/Records** – The Processor keeps documents proving they have complied with these clauses and allows the Controller to audit them to see that they are complying with the clauses.[184]

I refer to these clauses as the GDPR Processor clauses.

[180] GDPR – Article 28(3)(d)

[181] GDPR – Article 28(3)(e)

[182] GDPR – Article 28(3)(f)

[183] GDPR – Article 28(3)(g)

[184] GDPR – Article 28(3)(h)

Let's talk about Sub-Processors

Sometimes your company will use a Processor and that Processor will use a Sub-Processor to help them with the processing operations.

For example:

- Top Bank stores its customer data in the cloud.
- It uses Black Cloud, a cloud provider, to store the data on their cloud systems.
- Top Bank is a Controller and Black Cloud is a Processor.
- Black Cloud use some cloud providers of their own to help them store Top Bank's data.
- Black Cloud need consent from Top Bank to use these new Sub-Processor cloud providers to help them to store the data.

If a Processor uses a Sub-Processor to help them then they must:

- Obtain the general or specific consent of the Controller.
- Advise the Controller of any changes to the Sub-Processors they use.
- Sign the Sub-Processor up to all of the clauses from (a)-(h) above.

This can be a difficult thing for a Controller to keep an eye on as they are not going to know too much about all of the various Sub-Processors that the Processor might hire.

What kind of consent is needed from a Processor to use a Sub-Processor? Processors are starting to use a general consent rather than a specific consent.

There are different forms of consent.

Using the example above, Top Bank stores its customer data in the cloud. It uses Black Cloud, a cloud provider, to store the data on their cloud systems. Top Bank is a Controller and Black Cloud is a Processor. Black

Cloud use some cloud providers of their own to help them store Top Bank's data. They need consent to use these new Sub-Processor cloud providers to help them to store the data.

They do not tell Top Bank and all their Controllers individually every time they change a Sub-Processor. Instead, they publish a list on their website of the Sub-Processors they use and they allow their Controllers to view this list if they want to know. Whilst this might not be the ideal form of 'consent', many companies find it to be a workable solution.

What happens if the Processor does not agree to the clauses?

These clauses are very important because you, as a Controller, will be in breach of GDPR if they are not included in your contracts. It is up to the Controller (not the Processor) to make sure the clauses are in place.

Sometimes, Processors will not agree to these clauses.

You must take a risk-based decision on whether you want to proceed with that Processor based on the amount and sensitivity of the data you are sharing.

If the Processor loses your data or if a regulator ever asks you about the arrangement, then you could be in potential trouble. It is strongly recommended to put these clauses in place.

Are these the only clauses you should include?

It makes sense to ask your Processor to include additional clauses that will help you manage the risks for you.

For example, you may wish to include clauses relating to:

- **Indemnities** – The Processor will indemnify you for loss and damage if they are ever responsible for a data breach in respect of personal data. If you are a Controller, then you will want to make the Processor liable for as much of the loss that flows from a data breach as you can. For example, you may want an indemnity to cover you against loss, damage and expense caused by the Processor's data breach.

- **Cyber Insurance** – The Processor will maintain cyber insurance so they can cover any losses resulting from a data breach so they can pay the bill if they cause any loss to you.

These clauses are very important in managing your financial risk.

Can you ask the Processor to indemnify you against GDPR fines?

Sometimes companies ask their Processors to include clauses in the contact saying that the Processor will cover the cost of any GDPR fines that the Controller faces if the GDPR breach is caused by the Processor. These clauses are generally unenforceable in law so if they are included in a contract and the Controller is later fined by a Regulator, then it is unlikely that the Controller could recover the cost of the fine from the Processor.

To audit or not to audit?

You will see that you have a right to audit under the GDPR Processor clauses at Article 28.

Should you audit your Processors? If you have many hundreds of Processors, then you will not have time to show up at their premises to audit them all! Sometimes, it is best to audit your Processors in more indirect ways such as through asking them if you can see the results of other times they were audited themselves by third parties.

Some of my contracts with Processors pre-date GDPR? Do I have to put the GDPR clauses in?

You are required to insert the GDPR Processor clauses in respect of all of your contracts with Processors. You may want to start with the higher risk contracts, such as those processing large amounts of personal data or sensitive personal data.

Do Processors outside the EEA and UK have to sign up to the GDPR Processor clauses?

If your company is a Controller and is subject to GDPR, then you should get your Processors to sign up to the GDPR Processor clauses, regardless of where they are in the world.

Cloud Contracts

Often cloud providers are Processors. They have a tendency to offer their services on a 'take it or leave it' basis. They may not have the GDPR Processor Clauses in place. If you are handing over large amounts of personal data to a cloud provider, then you are taking a substantial risk if they do not have the clauses in place.

Is there room for negotiation?

Yes. Try to make sure your company has the most protection possible from the contract with the Processor. Sometimes, there is room for manoeuvre in some aspects of the contract. The Processor may agree to some of your demands and not others. It is important that they have the GDPR Processor Clauses in the contract. (See para above '**What clauses must we put in the Processor contract?**').

Processors, particularly if they are powerful processors, may not always agree to the GDPR Processor Clauses. Be aware that this leaves your company exposed.

Part B – Contracts between Controllers

The rules on contracts differ if you are sharing personal data with another Controller, instead of a Processor.

For example, Gold Insurance are working with an insurance underwriter called BDML. Both Gold Insurance and BDML are Controllers. They do not have to put the GDPR Processor Clauses in place under Article 28 of GDPR. However, it makes sense for them to put other clauses in place, setting out the rules of the game in terms of how the personal data will be processed.

Contracts between a Controller and other Controllers are called Data Sharing Agreements.

The ICO says "*it is good practice to have a data sharing agreement....having a data sharing agreement in place helps you to demonstrate you are meeting your accountability obligations under GDPR*".[185]

Contracts between Joint Controllers

Joint Controllers is where two controllers are acting together in a joint manner in respect of the data processing.

For example, two insurance companies work together to build a joint marketing database that they both can use to cross-sell to each other's customers.

The ICO has said that "If you are acting with another controller as joint controllers of personal data, there is a legal obligation to set out your responsibilities in a joint control arrangement, under both the UK GDPR/Part 2 of the DPA 2018 and under Part 3 of the DPA 2018...... a data sharing agreement could help you to put a joint control arrangement in place."[186]

A Data Sharing Agreement should be put in place for Joint Controllers.

What should the Data Sharing Agreement between the Controllers or Joint Controllers include?

There is no prescribed format for the issues that must be included in Data Sharing Agreements.

[185] ICO Data Sharing Code of Practice – 17 December 2020 – Page 25

[186] ICO Data Sharing Code of Practice – 17 December 2020 – Page 27

The ICO suggests [187]you should include the following:

1. **Who are the parties to the agreement?**
2. **What is the purpose of the data sharing?**
3. **Which other organisations will be involved in the data sharing?**
4. **What types of data are you going to share?**
5. **What is our lawful basis for sharing?**
6. **What about access and individual rights?** This data sharing agreement may set out who is responsible for the various GDPR obligations, such as dealing with Data Subject Access Requests and who is the contact point for data subjects.
7. **What information governance arrangements should we have?** For example, how do you ensure the data is kept accurate and up to date? How do you ensure it is deleted in a timely manner?

How often should contracts be reviewed?

Contracts should be reviewed regularly to ensure your Processors are behaving themselves when it comes to handling the personal data. Any substantial updates to the personal data processing should be added to the contract.

Similarly, Data Sharing Agreements between Controllers and Joint Controllers should also be reviewed and updated to reflect major changes.

Practical steps to take

1. **Supplier/Vendor Approval Process** – It makes sense to put a supplier approval process in place before you agree to sign up processors. You can put a questionnaire in place so that all new suppliers must answer questions (See para above **Vetting the**

[187] ICO Data Sharing Code of Practice – 17 December 2020 – Page 27

Processor) to show you that they are a reliable company and can be trusted with your customer data.

2. **Updating your contracts:**

    a. **New Contracts with Processors**– Work with your Legal Department to ensure that the GDPR Processor clauses are in place to cover the data processing between your company and all the Processor Suppliers you use. GDPR Processor Clauses from Article 28 of GDPR are a legal requirement.

    b. **New Contracts with other Controllers** – It is advisable to put contracts in place on Controller- Controller arrangements and Joint Controller arrangements.

    c. **Older contracts** – Begin to put the GDPR Processor clauses in to your pre-GDPR contracts by starting with the higher risk contracts.

3. **Audit** – Consider putting a procedure in place to regularly audit your existing contracts as you go forward. You can consider sending your suppliers questionnaires on a regular basis. The questionnaires should confirm that the personal data is sufficiently secure and that the Processor has not suffered any breach incidents etc.

CHAPTER ELEVEN

PROCESSING EMPLOYEE DATA

Introduction

This chapter sets out some of the basic issues relating to processing employee data. Whilst we cannot cover all of the issues relating to Data Protection and employment, we do set out some of the more important issues along with practical steps you can take in order to stay compliant.

Financial Services companies will hold all sorts of employee data including:

- Employee emails
- Personnel file
- Work history
- Sickness records
- CCTV footage
- Background checks
- Benefits information
- Information from employee monitoring tools (see below)

The Data Protection Principles

Firms must ensure they are processing employee data in line with the Data Protection Principles. The principles touch upon many aspects of data processing. A brief example of how each principle may have an impact on employee data appears below:

1. **Lawfulness, fairness and transparency**

Employers must be clear with employees about how their data is used in Staff Privacy Notices and Staff Handbooks.

2. **Purpose limitation**

Firms cannot collect employee data for one purpose and then go behind the employee's back to use it for an entirely different purpose. For example, if data is collected for staff administration, then it cannot be used for data analytics or marketing.

3. **Data minimisation**

Employers should not collect more data than they need from employees or job applicants.

4. **Accuracy**

Firms should take reasonable steps to ensure the data they retain on employees is accurate and they should allow employees to update it.

5. **Storage limitation**

Firms should draw up Data Retention Schedules to set out how long employee data is retained.

6. **Security**

There should be appropriate security around employee data, particularly in relation to health or sickness data. Firms should check and confirm that the controls in this area are sufficient. For example, do not assume that all HR employees should be allowed to access all employee data. Restrict access to employee records to those who need to see them.

7. **Accountability**

HR should keep records of the processing.

Legal basis for processing employee data

In order to process any employee data, then one of the following grounds under Article 6 of GDPR must apply.

Which is the most appropriate legal basis for processing employee data? These appear below:

Contractual necessity – It is likely that much of the typical data processing done on employee data will be necessary under the employment contract. For example, staff administration and payroll processing are likely to be necessary under the contract.

Legitimate interests of the employer – Much employee personal data processing will be within the legitimate interests of the employer. For example, some employers may find they have a legitimate interest to put CCTV cameras at the front of their offices. If this is necessary and in their legitimate interest and if it does not override the fundamental rights and freedoms of the employee (e.g. it does not collect data excessively), then this is a valid legal basis.

Legal obligation – Employers must pass employee details to the tax authorities such as the HMRC because they are under a legal obligation to do so. The ICO has said "*The employer can point to the HMRC website where the requirements are set out to demonstrate this obligation. In this situation it is not necessary to cite each specific piece of legislation.*"[188]

Consent – Consent often does not work in an employment context because there is an imbalance in the relationship between employers and employees. Employers hold the power in the relationship which means that it could be hard for an employer to show that the consent was freely given.

There are some circumstances in which employers could rely on consent if it can be shown that the employee gave it freely.

For example, Big Bank hold a competition for employees. Big Bank want employees to help them improve efficiency in the company. They organise a competition for employees: The employee who suggests the best money saving idea wins a free meal in a nearby restaurant. Dave decides to enter the competition. Big Bank can rely on consent here to process Dave's data as part of the competition because Dave is entering the competition voluntarily and he is under no pressure to do so.

188 ICO.org.uk – Legal Obligation

See Chapter 1 for more details on the lawful bases for processing personal data.

Processing special category data in an employment context

We have discussed the processing of special category data in Chapter 1.

Processing special category data under GDPR is not easy. You must comply with the requirements under GDPR and under the Data Protection Act 2018.

If your firm is processing special category data on employees such as personal data relating to race, politics, religion, genetics, biometrics, health, sex life or sexuality, then you will need one of the legal bases we have set out above. You will also need a further legal basis under Article 9 of GDPR.

For example, Premium Insurance company collect personal data relating to their employees' race and religion so they can carry out equal opportunities monitoring.

This table below sets out some of the Article 9 legal basis that may be most appropriate in an employment context.

Legal basis under GDPR Article 9 (2) for processing special category personal data under GDPR	**More detail**
(a) Explicit consent	The employee has given explicit consent to the processing of the personal data. For example, some employers seek explicit consent to conduct employee monitoring.
(b) Employment law legal obligation	Processing is necessary for the purposes of carrying out the obligations in the field of employment law. For example, some employers process employee data because they have an employment law obligation to do so.[189]

[189] Also at Data Protection Act 2018 – Part 1, Schedule 1, Para 1

	A company may process employee special category personal data under an employment law legal obligation e.g. processing employee data for statutory sickness records.
(f) Legal claims and judicial acts	Processing is necessary for the establishment, exercise or defence of legal claims. For example, processing the personal data in the context of defending an employee's legal claim against your company.
(g) Substantial public interest conditions	Processing is necessary for reasons of substantial public interest. If you are relying on this condition, then you will need a further legal basis under the Data Protection Act 2018. See Chapter 1 for more details.

Criminal Offence Data

Be very careful when processing criminal offence data relating to employees. You should avoid processing criminal offence data if at all possible.

To process criminal offence data, you must have a ground under a) and b):

a) Have a legal basis under Article 6 of GDPR, and

b) Comply with Schedule 1, Part 1 of the Data Protection Act 2018.

One of the grounds under b. that might fit in an employment context is:

'The processing is necessary for the purposes of performing or exercising obligations or rights which are imposed or conferred by law on the controller or the data subject in connection with employment'. [190]

Always complete a Data Protection Impact Assessment form (DPIA) to try to mitigate the Data Protection Risks before processing any criminal data relating to employees.

190 Data Protection Act 2018 – Part 1, Schedule 1, Para 1

Criminal offence for a company to force an employee to make a Data Subject Access Request

It is a criminal offence for an employer to force an individual to make an Access Request for their records e.g. if a prospective employer forces a candidate to apply to the police for their criminal record. [191]

Employee monitoring

What is employee monitoring?

Employee monitoring is becoming more prevalent in companies. Employers often monitor:

- Employee use of their computer systems
- How long employees spend on particular applications, such as Outlook
- Phone usage
- Employee entry into the building via CCTV
- Online behaviour via cookies

There are many technologies/software applications that conduct employee monitoring.

The employer should be able to show that the monitoring is necessary and proportionate.

For example:

- Dodgy Insurance want to record all calls made from their telephone systems by all 1,000 of their employees.

[191] Data Protection Act 2018 – s184

- Dodgy think that listening to employee calls might be interesting and they have a suspicion that one of their employees might be defrauding them.
- This is not compliant with GDPR because Dodgy are unable to show that it is necessary to conduct this level of monitoring.
- It is also disproportionate to monitor the entire workforce in this way due to a suspicion concerning just one employee.

Tips on employee monitoring:

- **DPIA** – If employee monitoring is to be conducted, then a Data Protection Impact Assessment (DPIA) form should be completed.
- **Legal Basis** – An appropriate legal basis must be in place for the monitoring. If the monitoring processes special category data or criminal data, then you must comply with the rules in these areas. It is much harder to make a case for monitoring that involves special category data or criminal data.
- **Targeted** – Monitoring should be targeted as much as possible. Do not monitor the entire workforce when you can use less intrusive means, such as spot checks, to conduct monitoring.
- **Transparency** – Be transparent with employees about how monitoring is conducted in Privacy Notices.

Employees and profiling

The Right to have human oversight in a decision made by a computer

Under GDPR, employees have a right to have human oversight in a decision that has been made by a computer. [192]

For example, Clare works for Golden Boys Asset Managers. She is advised that she can apply for a promotion at work. She completes the online application form. Two weeks later, she receives an email advising that her application has been refused. When she asks about this, Golden tell her that a computer reviews the applications. Clare has the right to ask Golden to review her application again and this time, to ask a human being to look at the data, as well as the computer.

Companies must ensure that employees can:

- obtain human oversight or intervention in the decision, and
- express their point of view, and
- receive an explanation of the decision and challenge it.

If you do use software tools that make decisions about employees or job applicants, then you should make sure some human review is built-in to any decision that the software tool makes.

Training Employees on Data Protection and GDPR

It is important to ensure employees are properly trained on Data Protection, including their obligations under GDPR.

It is recommended that employees should receive a general Data Protection training session at least once a year. This should set out the basic rules under GDPR, including advice on how to keep personal data safe. Many financial services companies ask employees to complete an online Data Protection training module online. Companies can purchase these modules for employees.

---

[192] GDPR – Article 22

Some sectors of your organisation may require further Data Protection Training over and above the general Data Protection Training.

For example:

- Marketing – The Marketing Team should be trained on the rules relating to consents, electronic marketing and buying personal data.
- IT Security – IT Security should be trained on the expectations within GDPR on keeping data safe.

Staff Privacy Notices

Companies must set out how they process personal data in their Staff Privacy Notice that is available on the company's intranet page. It should advise your employees of the specifics in relation to their personal data processing including:

- The data that is collected about them
- Any profiling that is conducted
- Employee monitoring
- Who it is shared with
- Where it is transported
- How long it is kept

Your company likely already has a Staff Privacy Notice. You may want to check it to see that it covers all relevant areas.

See Chapter 12 for more details on Privacy Notices.

Recruitment

Companies must ensure they are compliant with the GDPR in relation to the recruitment process.

Some issues to consider:

- **Transparency** – Try to ensure that job applicants have sufficient privacy information when they are applying for a job. For example, ensure your Privacy Policy is readily available for applicants when they are applying for a job online. See Chapter 12 for more details on Privacy Notices.
- **Excessive Data** – Ensure that your job application forms do not collect more personal information than you need.
- **Profiling** – Computer applications should not reject applicants for jobs without a human being involved at some point in the decision-making process.
- **Forced DSAR** – It is a criminal offence to force an individual to make an Access Request for their records e.g. if a prospective employer forces a candidate to apply to the police for their criminal record.

Conclusion and Practical steps to consider when processing Employee Personal Data

1. **Audit** – Audit your HR Team to understand the personal data processing that is ongoing. Send questionnaires to HR to gain an understanding of their data processing. You can ask HR to answer questions such as:
   - The categories of personal data processed
   - How the data is processed
   - Whether special category or criminal data is being processed
   - How long the data is kept for
   - Who within HR has access
   - What Data Protection Training do they receive
   - What kind of monitoring is conducted

2. **Training** – Train staff on GDPR and Data Protection Training at least annually, with further specific training for individual departments such as Marketing, IT and HR.

3. **Legal bases** – Consider whether the legal bases you have in place for processing employee data are appropriate and keep records of this.

4. **Staff Privacy Policy** – Firms are also expected to have "appropriate data protection policies" in place.[193] A staff policy is an instruction manual to employees, setting out how they must handle personal data. You should put a policy in place advising employees what their obligations are in respect of processing personal data. A staff policy is important in complying with your Article 5 GDPR accountability obligations.[194]

5. **Staff Privacy Notice** – A Privacy Notice tells employees how and why their personal data is processed. Staff Privacy Notices usually appear on your company website and often, they are also included in Staff handbooks. To be fully transparent with employees, your company needs a Staff Privacy Notice, telling them how and why you process their personal data. Check your Staff Privacy Notice to ensure it covers the important points of your personal data processing.

6. **Data Protection Impact Assessments** – Ensure DPIAs are completed for any risky processing, including all instances of employee monitoring.

---

[193] GDPR – Article 24(2)

[194] 1. Also, the Data Protection Act 2018 (DPA 2018) outlines the requirement for an Appropriate Policy Document (APD) to be in place when processing special category and criminal offence data under certain specified conditions.

CHAPTER TWELVE

FURTHER GDPR RULES

There are a number of other rules under GDPR that are very relevant to companies in the financial services sector.

Your company is likely to have a Privacy Program in place to meet many of its GDPR obligations. The content of this chapter aims to provide a brief reminder of some of the other more administrative rules relating to GDPR.

Data Protection Officers – Who are they?

The DPO is supposed to act as a mini in-house regulator at your company, keeping it on the right side of Data Protection.

The law on Data Protection Officers (DPOs) appears at Article 37, 38 and 39 of GDPR.

A company (including Processors and Controllers) must appoint a DPO if its:

- Core activities require regular and systematic monitoring of data subjects on a large scale, OR
- Core activities consist of the processing of special categories of data or criminal data on a large scale.[195]

Your company may wish to appoint a DPO even if it is not obliged to do so. If it does appoint a DPO then the DPO is subject to all the rules under GDPR on DPOs (GDPR Articles 37-39).

[195] GDPR – Article 37(1)(b) and (c)

If your company is a group of companies, then it may appoint a single Data Protection Officer to serve all the companies in the Group, as long as the DPO 'is easily accessible' from each establishment.[196]

The DPO should have 'expert knowledge of data protection law' and the ability to fulfil their obligations under GDPR.[197]

The company should give the DPO the appropriate amount of resources to carry out their tasks. [198] The DPO is also entitled to a certain amount of independence in that he or she "*shall not receive any instructions regarding the exercise of those tasks*" and the company "*shall ensure that any such tasks and duties do not result in a conflict of interests*".[199]

What does the DPO do?

The DPO has a number of tasks including:

- Advising your company on GDPR obligations
- Monitoring compliance with GDPR
- Advising on DPIAs
- Dealing with EU Supervisory Authorities[200]
- Being the contact point on personal data for customers and employees[201]
- Managing Data Protection risks[202]

---

[196] GDPR – Article 37(2)

[197] GDPR – Article 37(5)

[198] GDPR – Article 38(2)

[199] GDPR – Article 38(3) and (6)

[200] GDPR – Article 39

[201] GDPR – Article – 38(4)

[202] GDPR – Article 39(2)

Remedies under GDPR

Data subjects can sue a Processor or a Controller for compensation under GDPR. They do not have to prove that they have suffered monetary loss or damage[203]. Data subjects can sue for distress or inconvenience.[204]

Data Protection Authorities

Each EU member state has its own Data Protection Authority. The UK has its own Data Protection Authority called the Information Commissioner's Officer (ICO). Throughout this book, you will see them referred to as 'Regulators'.

The Regulators have a number of powers including:

Investigative powers – This includes the power to carry out audits and to get access to a company's premises.[205]

Corrective powers – This includes the power to issue fines and to order a Controller to comply with an order. Regulators can even ban a company from processing personal data.[206]

Authorisation and advisory powers – This includes the power to advise a Controller, to approve a company's application for Binding Corporate Rules, to authorise high risk processing. [207]

Fines under GDPR

Regulators do not have an unfettered right to fine. Fines must be 'proportionate'[208] and potentially, a company could bring a legal court challenge to a Regulator's fine, if they held the fine to be

---

[203] GDPR – Article 82(1)

[204] ICO.org.uk – Taking your case to court and claiming compensation

[205] GDPR – Article 58(1)

[206] GDPR – Article 58(2)

[207] GDPR – Article 58(3)

[208] GDPR – Article 83(1)

disproportionate. Before a fine is officially issued, a company will receive a Notice of Intention to fine in a certain amount. In practical terms, if a company does receive a Notice of Intention to fine, then it is best advised to work with the Regulator and to try to persuade the Regulator to keep the fine level down, by showing the Regulator that it has seen the error of its ways and improved its processes.

There are two tiers of fines:

a. **2 % of total worldwide turnover or 10 million (whichever is higher)** – Including for breaches of any Design and Default Rules, The Processor Contract Rules, the DPIA rules, Records of Processing Rules, the Data Protection Officer Rules.[209]

b. **4 % of total worldwide turnover or 20 million (whichever is higher)** – Including for breaches of the Data Protection Principles, Lawful bases conditions, Data Subject Rights and Transfer Rules.[210]

Privacy Notices

The first principle of Data Protection says that companies must process personal data fairly, lawfully and transparently.

Companies must have a clear and concise Privacy Notice that uses plain language, telling data subjects how their personal data is processed.[211]

Privacy Notices are usually provided on a company's website, but they can also be provided in paper form, [212]such as in documentation that a customer receives from his or her insurance company.

---

[209] GDPR – Article 83(4)

[210] GDPR – Article 83(5)

[211] GDPR – Article 12(1)

[212] GDPR – Article 12(1)

What information should Privacy Notices include?

The ICO explains the information your company must provide in its Privacy Notice in the table below:

What information do we need to provide?	Personal data collected from individuals	Personal data obtained from other sources
The name and contact details of your organisation	✓	✓
The name and contact details of your representative	✓	✓
The contact details of your data protection officer	✓	✓
The purposes of the processing	✓	✓
The lawful basis for the processing	✓	✓
The legitimate interests for the processing	✓	✓
The categories of personal data obtained		✓
The recipients or categories of recipients of the personal data	✓	✓

The details of transfers of the personal data to any third countries or international organisations	✓	✓
The retention periods for the personal data	✓	✓
The rights available to individuals in respect of the processing	✓	✓
The right to withdraw consent	✓	✓
The right to lodge a complaint with a supervisory authority	✓	✓
The source of the personal data		✓
The details of whether individuals are under a statutory or contractual obligation to provide the personal data	✓	
The details of the existence of automated decision-making, including profiling	✓	✓

When you do collect the personal data directly from the data subject, then you must provide the Privacy Notice information at the time the data is collected.[213]

When you do **not** collect the personal data directly from the data subject, then you must provide the Privacy Notice information "within one month" at the latest.[214]

There are some exemptions to providing Privacy Notice information, including where the data subject already has the information. These exemptions are set out at Articles 13(4) and 14(5) of GDPR.

Records of Processing

Under Article 30 of GDPR, Controllers with 250 or more employees, are expected to keep records of their processing (known as 'ROPs') activities including:

a) the name and contact details of the company

b) the purposes of the processing

c) a description of the categories of data subjects and of the categories of personal data

d) the categories of recipients to whom the personal data has been or will be disclosed, including recipients in third countries or international organisations

e) where applicable, transfers of personal data to third countries

f) where possible, the envisaged time limits for erasure of the different categories of data

g) where possible, a general description of the security in place in relation to the data

---

[213] GDPR – Article 13(1)

[214] GDPR – Article 14(3)(a)

Processors are also expected to keep records of their personal data processing. [215]

Companies are exempt from putting ROPs in place if they have fewer than 250 employees, see Article 30 of GDPR for more details. [216]

It can take time putting ROPs in place because companies are expected to carry out a data audit to find out where all of their data resides.

Web forms or spreadsheets that capture these details in a consistent manner across your business should be put in place. Failure to comply with ROP obligations can attract fines of 10 million or 2% of global turnover.[217]

EU Representative

There are some rules at Article 27 of GDPR that must be considered.

A. Some companies are caught by EU GDPR, but they are not physically in the EU.

These companies must appoint a legal entity, such as a company in the EU, to be their EU Representative. In other words, the company will be their contact point should a Regulator in the EU or a data subject in the EU want to get in touch with them easily.

B. Some companies are caught by UK GDPR, but they are not physically in the UK.

These companies must appoint a legal entity, such as a company, to be their UK Representative. In other words, the company will be their contact point should a Regulator in the UK or a data subject in the UK want to get in touch with them easily.

There are some exceptions to the rules on appointing representatives, such as where the processing is only occasional and does not involve

---

[215] GDPR – Article 30(1) and (2)

[216] GDPR – Article 30(5)

[217] GDPR – Article 83(4)

special category personal data and is unlikely to result in risk to individuals. See Article 27 for more details.

Data Protection by Design

Under Article 25 of GDPR, companies are expected to take appropriate steps to bake data protection compliance into their data processing from the outset.

For example, Big Bank is starting a new data analytics project, using their customer data. The purpose of the project is to provide insight into their customer spending habits. Big Bank will be expected to bake data protection compliance into the plan right from the beginning of the project. Big Bank must ensure that principles such as Data Minimisation (using the least amount of personal data necessary) are implemented from the start of the project and all the way through to its conclusion.[218]

Data Protection by Default

The EC Commission has said *"By default, companies/organisations should ensure that personal data is processed with the highest privacy protection (for example only the data necessary should be processed, short storage period, limited accessibility) so that by default personal data isn't made accessible to an indefinite number of persons ('data protection by default')."*

For example *"A social media platform should be encouraged to set users' profile settings in the most privacy-friendly setting by, for example, limiting from the start the accessibility of the users' profile so that it isn't accessible by default to an indefinite number of persons."*[219]

---

[218] GDPR – Article 25

[219] European Commission Website – What does data protection 'by design' and 'by default' mean?

Cookies

The rules on cookies are set out in the EU E-Privacy Directive and the UK PECR Regulations. GDPR is also in play if the cookies process personal data.

The ICO states, *"A cookie is a small text file that is downloaded onto 'terminal equipment' (eg a computer or smartphone) when the user accesses a website. It allows the website to recognise that user's device and store some information about the user's preferences or past actions.*

What do we need to do to comply?

The rules on cookies are in regulation 6. The basic rule is that you must:

- *tell people the cookies are there;*
- *explain what the cookies are doing and why; and*
- *get the person's consent to store a cookie on their device."*[220]

Cookies must not be installed until the company has obtained the appropriate consent from the website user. They must provide enough information on the site near the cookie consent to explain how the cookie data is processed.

The consent required is the GDPR standard of consent under Article 7. It must be freely given, specific, informed and one must opt in.[221]

Policies

There are some legal requirements under GDPR to put staff policies in place to explain to staff what their responsibilities are in relation to personal data. Article 24 demands that companies have "appropriate data protection policies" in place.

[220] Ico.org.uk – Cookies and similar technologies

[221] GDPR – Article 4(11), Article 7

There are also legal requirements under the Data Protection Act 2018 to have policies in place if you process criminal data or special category data.[222]

Policies are really just about common sense. They help your employees understand what the rules are in terms of handling personal data.

There are many templates available on the ICO's website in relation to Data Protection Policies.

Writing the policies is the easy part. What you really want to do as a company is to embed the policies in your operations.

This includes:

- Telling your employees about your policies in your staff training.
- Making staff read and acknowledge the fact that they have read and understood your policies regularly.
- Updating your policies annually.
- Disciplining employees who break your policies.

At a minimum, a financial services company consider putting the following policies in place:

- **Data Protection Policy** – The basic rules on handling personal data.
- **Records Management Policy including Records Retention Schedule** – The policy detailing the time periods after which different types of data should be deleted.

[222] **Ico.org.uk – should we document anything else?** "*in the UK, the DPA 2018 sets out several conditions for the processing of special category or criminal conviction and offence data. To satisfy several of these conditions, you must have a policy document that details your procedures for complying with the principles in Article 5 of the UK GDPR and sets out your policies for retaining and erasing the special category / criminal conviction and offence data.*"

- **Cloud Policy** – The policy governing how the company is to use cloud services and cloud providers to ensure that data is processed securely.
- **Personal Data Breach Incident Policy** – The rules on handling company personal data breaches.
- **Encryption Policy** – The rules on how encryption is to be used when data is in transit and at rest.
- **Outsourcing Policy** – The policy governing how suppliers are to be chosen and how due diligence is to be conducted to ensure they keep personal data entrusted to them safe.
- **Data Subject Rights Policy and Procedure** – The Policy setting out how the company will maintain compliance with data subject requests under GDPR.

Practical steps to take:

1. **Data Audit** – Consider a company-wide Data Audit, to try to understand how data is processed within your company. Use your data audit to ascertain:
    - The type of data you hold.
    - Details on how you collect the personal data eg directly from the customer or from other sources.
    - The categories of data subjects on whom you hold personal data.
    - How it is processed e.g. for HR purposes, marketing, data analytics, insurance underwriting.
    - The security that is used in relation to the personal data.
    - Details on who is allowed to access the data.
    - The lawful bases in place for processing your personal data.

- The international transfers made in relation to the personal data.
- The level of complaints you receive in respect of personal data processing.
- The marketing you conduct using personal data.
- The level of training employees receive.
- How and when the personal data is deleted.
- The entities with whom you share the personal data.

It makes sense to draw up questionnaires in relation to the personal data processing you conduct and then to send the questionnaires to your central functions such as HR, IT Security, Legal Internal Audit, Finance and Marketing. You should also send the questionnaires to your individual Business Units and sister companies.

Once you have identified the higher risk areas of your data processing, you can act to put better controls in place to bring you into compliance with GDPR.

2. **Privacy Notices** – Privacy Notices tell individuals such as your customers about how you process personal data. Review your company's Privacy Notices to see if there are any additions that need to be made.

3. **Staff Policies** – Assess whether you need to add any further policies to your list of current policies, governing security and Data Protection within your company. Update policies where appropriate. Ensure employees read and acknowledge each of your policies annually. Include reference to your policies in your Annual Data Protection training.

4. **Records of Processing** – Set up a Record of Processing process within your company and ask that each entity within your company completes a ROP regularly.

5. **EU Representatives** – Appoint EU and UK Representatives if necessary.
6. **Cookies** – Check your websites to ensure appropriate cookie notices and consents are in place.

CHAPTER THIRTEEN
GDPR RIGHTS IN FINANCIAL SERVICES

GDPR is a rights regulation. It gives individuals control over their personal data and how it is processed.

Financial services companies process personal data on all sorts of individuals including:

- Customers
- Employees
- Contractors
- Marketing prospects
- Sole traders
- Members of the public filmed on CCTV
- Individuals who are tracked via the company's website

All of these individuals have certain rights over personal information that your company holds on them:

1. The right of access
2. The right to rectification
3. The right to erasure
4. The right to restrict processing
5. The right to data portability
6. The right to object
7. Rights in relation to automated decision making and profiling.

Rights can be difficult and expensive for companies to deal with. We are going to look at each right in turn. We will look at some practical steps for dealing with GDPR rights at the conclusion of the chapter.

Rights requests – the formalities

a) **Must be answered within one month** – GDPR Rights Requests must be responded to "within one month". [223]

b) **Customers can make a request by email, letter or on the phone** [224]- They can be made in any format including orally, by email or even to your company via Twitter. Individuals do not have to complete your company Access Request or Erasure form for a request to be valid. They can make a request in any format they choose.

c) **Companies usually must deal with these requests** – A company can only refuse to act on a request if it is:

    - Manifestly unfounded, or
    - Manifestly excessive [225].

d) **Check the person's identity** – Companies should use "all reasonable measures" to verify the identity of people making GDPR rights requests.[226] In other words, you should take reasonable steps to verify the person's identity before complying with their request.

---

[223] GDPR – Article 12(3)

[224] GDPR – Article 12(3)

[225] GDPR – Article 12(5)

[226] GDPR – Recital 64

Part 1 – The Right of Access

Access Requests – Introduction

Individuals have a Right of Access over their personal data. This allows them to make what is referred to as a Data Subject Access Request (also known as a 'DSAR' or an 'Access Request'). We are going to use the term Access Request for ease of reference.

Access Requests are very powerful. When an individual is having a dispute with a company, then making an Access Request can put the company on the back foot.

The Right of Access is the most prominent right under GDPR. In fact, the ICO receive more complaints about Access Requests than any other issue.

Access Requests can be very expensive for companies to deal with. One recent study showed that Access Requests can cost companies up to £1.58 million per year to deal with.[227]

Under Access Requests, individuals are allowed to receive access to and a copy of their personal data.[228]

The motive of the person making the access request is largely irrelevant. [229] It doesn't matter what their motive is. You must provide the data to them.

For example, Ashley Hudd is having a dispute with her bank. Ashley thinks she has been overcharged by her bank for a number of services. Ashley makes an Access Request for all her personal data because she wants to view the data to see if she might have a legal case against her bank. Ashley is allowed to access her data. Her motives for accessing the data are irrelevant.

---

[227] Guardum Study 2020

[228] GDPR – Article 15(3)

[229] Dawson-Damer & Ors v. Taylor Wessing LLP [2017] EWCA Civ 91

Access Requests – Supplementary Information

What other information is an individual entitled to?

In addition to a copy of their personal data, the individual making the request is also entitled to other supplementary information[230], such as details on:

a) the purposes of your processing i.e. why you are doing the processing.

b) the categories of personal data concerned i.e. what kinds of personal data elements you are processing.

c) the recipients or categories of recipient to whom the personal data has been or will be disclosed to i.e. information about who you are sharing the personal data with.

d) your retention period for storing the personal data or, where this is not possible, your criteria for determining how long you will store it i.e. how long you are keeping the personal data before deleting it.

e) the existence of their right to request rectification, erasure or restriction or to object to such processing i.e. the other rights they are entitled to assert under GDPR.

f) the right to lodge a complaint with the ICO or another supervisory authority.

g) information about the source of the data, where it was not obtained directly from the individual i.e. where or from who, you obtained the data.

h) the existence of automated decision-making (including profiling) i.e. whether any computer is making a decision about the data subject.

---

[230] GDPR – Article 15(1)

i) the safeguards you provide if you transfer personal data to a third country or international organisation i.e. whether you are sending the personal data outside the EU or UK.

a) – i) is the Supplementary Information. Most companies provide a copy of the documents and only provide the Supplementary Information if they are specifically asked for it.

More on Access Requests

Companies should train their staff to recognise Access Requests. Individuals making requests do not have to use the term Access Request or DSAR for it to be a valid request. If an individual says "I want all my data" then that counts as a valid Access Request.

Your company should search across its systems to find personal data relating to the data subject including emails, paper records, databases and archived data (if it has not been put beyond use).

Much of the personal data you find on a person making an Access Request ('a requestor') will include the data of third parties. For example, the data of Person A is likely to be mixed in with the data of Person B.

If it is not feasible to delete or edit the third-party data from a specific data set, such as a call recording or an email, **then you can refuse to release the third-party data to the requestor unless**:

1. The third party has consented to the document being released, or
2. It is reasonable to disclose the third-party data without consent.[231]

It is a criminal offence to try to hide or alter personal data on your systems to prevent it from being disclosed as part of an Access Request. [232]

[231] Data Protection Act 2018 – Schedule 2, Part 3 Paragraph 16

[232] Data Protection Act 2018 – s173

Access Requests – How should personal data be sent out?

GDPR says *"where the data subject makes the request by electronic means, and unless otherwise requested by the data subject, the information shall be provided in a commonly used electronic form."*[233] When you receive the request by email, it is best to reply using secure email.

GDPR suggests that Controllers should provide access via a secure portal, where possible.[234]

Can the company charge a fee for complying with an Access Request?

The company can charge a "reasonable fee" for "administrative costs" such as printing and copying if the data subject wants further copies.[235] This is often more trouble than it is worth.

Access Requests Exemptions

There are some exemptions to Access Requests that can permit companies to desist from providing personal data to individuals. The exemptions most relevant to financial services include:

1. **Crime and Taxation**[236] – For example, if releasing the data could prejudice a criminal investigation.
2. **Legal Professional Privilege**[237] – For example, if the data sought is subject to Legal Professional Privilege, such as data relating to legal advice received by a bank.

---

233 GDPR – Article 15(3)

234 GDPR – Recital 63

235 GDPR – Article 15(3)

236 Data Protection Act 2018, Sch 2, Part 1, para 2

237 Data Protection Act 2018, Sch 2, Part 4, para 19

3. **Management Forecasts**[238] – For example, if a bank was going to make an employee redundant and this had not yet been announced, then they may not have to release this data following the Access Request.

4. **Negotiations with the requestor**[239] – For example, if an employee was seeking a pay rise and he made an Access Request, then data relating to the negotiations may not have to be released following his Access Request.

5. **Confidential references**[240] – For example, if an employee made an Access Request and there was a confidential job reference relating to him, then it may not have to be released as part of the Access Request.

Be careful in using the exemptions. You should not use them in a blanket fashion. Rather you should decide whether they apply in a particular case. Take legal advice if you are unsure whether an exception applies to you. Always try to lean in favour of disclosing the personal data.

Part 2 – Further Rights Under GDPR

The Right to Erasure

Under the Right to Erasure, people have the right to erase their personal data but only in some circumstances. [241]

A person has the right to have their data erased in a number of cases including if:

- The data is no longer necessary for the purpose you had originally collected it for, or
- You were processing the person's data based on consent and they have now withdrawn that consent, or

[238] UK Data Protection Act 2018, Schedule 2, Part 4 para 22

[239] UK Data Protection Act 2018, Schedule 2, Part 4 para 23

[240] UK Data Protection Act 2018, Schedule 2, Part 4 para 24

[241] GDPR – Article 17

- The data has been processed unlawfully.

For example, Anna asked for a car insurance quote from Shifty Insurers ten years ago. When Anna phoned Shifty for a quotation, Shifty collected personal data relating to Anna's driving record and speeding convictions. Anna didn't like the price that was quoted and did not contact Shifty again. Anna heard that they were recently hacked and she decided to check that her data was deleted from their systems. Anna makes a Right to Erasure request for Shifty to delete her data and they agree to do so.

There are a number of exceptions to the Right to Erasure and I describe some of these immediately below. This means that a company could refuse to erase the person's data if they required the data for one of the following reasons:

- Complying with a legal obligation
- Defending a legal claim
- Public interest[242]

For example, Renee makes an erasure request against Shady Bank. Renee has been banking with Shady for 12 years. Shady hold some transaction data relating to payments Renee made. Renee wants all her data deleted because she no longer wants to bank with Shady. Shady retain the data and advise Renee that they are entitled to do this because they are complying with a legal obligation to retain certain data under the anti-money laundering regulations.

If you do receive a Right to Erasure request, you should consider whether the person has a valid request. You should also check whether any of the exceptions apply at Article 17(3) of GDPR which could prevent you from deleting the data.

[242] GDPR – Article 17(3)

The Right to Correct Personal Data

Under GDPR, individuals have the right to correct inaccurate personal data or to complete incomplete data about themselves.

For example, Dickens Insurance company receive a request to correct information from Ed. Ed has a car insurance policy with Dickens. Ed has noticed on his car insurance documentation that Dickens wrongly believes that Ed has 2 previous speeding convictions. Ed wants them to correct the record to reflect that he has only 1 previous conviction. Dickens agree to do this because Ed has made a valid Right to Correct Request.[243]

The Right to Restrict Processing

Under GDPR, individuals have a right to restrict processing. [244]This means that people can put a temporary hold on the way their personal data is processed until their complaint is resolved. In other words, people can ask you to stop doing whatever it is you are doing with their data whilst their complaint is being resolved. One can rely on this right if one of the following grounds applies:

a) the accuracy of the personal data is contested by the data subject.

b) the processing is unlawful and the data subject opposes the erasure of the personal data and requests the restriction of their use instead.

c) the Controller no longer needs the personal data for the purposes of the processing, but they are required by the data subject for the establishment, exercise or defence of legal claims.

For example, Chantelle opened an account with Mega Bank last month. Chantelle learns that Mega Insure are going to charge her a £100 fee because she used her overdraft facility. Mega Bank are going to proceed to take payment from Chantelle on 1 April. Chantelle disputes that she used her overdraft facility. She contends that Mega Bank are mistaken.

---

243 GDPR Article 16

244 GDPR – Article 18

Chantelle makes a request that Mega put a hold on processing the £100 fee until she investigates the matter further. Mega Bank agree to refrain from processing the payment until Chantelle investigates the matter.

The Right to Data Portability

This right could be quite widely used in financial services.

Under GDPR, people can have the personal data they have provided to a Controller sent to a new service provider in a 'structured, commonly used and machine-readable format'.

There is a caveat to the right in that an individual only has the right to ask for his or her data to be ported where it is "technically feasible".[245]

For example, Carl bought an apartment 5 years ago. He has been with the same mortgage provider, Gloom Mortgages, for all of that time. Carl gave Gloom Mortgages his consent to process his data when he applied for his mortgage 5 years ago. Carl wants to move to a new provider called Smile Mortgages. He asks Gloom to send his data to Smile. Gloom must transfer the data to Smile in a 'structured, commonly used and machine-readable format.' This means they must transfer it in a way that is easy for Smile to use, such as in a CSV file.

This right only applies where:

- The processing is based on consent.
- The processing is carried out by automated means.[246]

The Right to Object

Under GDPR, people have the right to object to their data being processed in a number of cases including when the Controller is relying on legitimate interests for the processing.

[245] GDPR – Article 20(2)

[246] GDPR – Article 20

For example, Jennie learns that Hilltop Insurance are relying on legitimate interests to process her data for the purposes of analytics. Jennie does not want analytics conducted on her personal data. She tells Hilltop that she objects to her data being used in this way. Hilltop stop processing Jennie's data for analytics purposes.

Under this right, individuals also have the right to object to their data being used for marketing purposes.

For example, Clive has been receiving marketing letters and emails from Bullion Bank for several months. Clive does not want to receive any more marketing material. He advises them that he no longer wishes to receive their marketing material. Bullion agree not to send any more marketing material.

The Right to have human oversight in a decision made by a computer

Under GDPR, people have a right to have human oversight in a decision that has been made by a computer. [247]For example, a decision by a computer that refuses you for a mortgage or refuses your application for a job.

For the person to rely on this right, the decision has to significantly affect the person. If companies do use computers to make decisions about individuals that significantly affect them, then they must ensure that individuals can:

- obtain human oversight or intervention in the decision, and
- express their point of view, and
- receive an explanation of the decision and challenge it.

For example, Jim wants to apply for a business loan for a new coffee shop. Jim applies to Brass Bank for a business loan. Brass Bank use a computer program to review loan applications. The computer application refuses Jim's application. Jim is distressed when he learns of this because he needs

[247] GDPR – Article 22

the loan immediately, otherwise the coffee shop will be in jeopardy. Jim demands that Brass Bank reconsider the application and to have a human involved in the process.

This right does not apply if the computer decision:

- is necessary for entering into, or performance of, a contract between the data subject and a data controller.
- is based on the data subject's explicit consent.[248]

Complying with the other rights

The table below helps set out the steps you must take if you receive a request relating to one of the GDPR rights.

Type of Right	Time Limit	Form request can be in	Search for the person's personal data	Actions to be taken	Provide a copy of the personal information
1. The Right of Access	Within one month	In any form e.g. email or orally	Search all of the company including emails, databases, systems. Asks processors to search too.	Review and consider third party data and whether exceptions apply. Consider Article 15 GDPR.	Provide copy.
2. The Right to Erasure	Within one month	In any form e.g. email or orally	Search for the data relating to the request.	Consider the exceptions. Delete data if appropriate. Consider Article 17 GDPR.	No,

[248] GDPR Article 22(2)

3. The Right to Correct Inaccurate Data	Within one month	In any form e.g. email or orally	View the data alleged as incorrect.	Consider whether inaccurate. Correct or update if necessary. Consider Article 16 GDPR.	No.
4. The Right to Restrict processing	Within one month	In any form e.g. email or orally	Consider the request to place a temporary hold on the data.	Consider whether temporary hold is appropriate. Stop processing the data if request is meritorious. Consider Article 18 GDPR.	No.
5. The Right to Data Portability	Within one month	In any form e.g. email or orally	Search all of the company including emails, databases, systems. Asks processors to search too.	If request has been made out, then put data on commonly used machine-readable file and send to new service provider. Consider Article 20 GDPR.	Provide copy to new service provider.
6. The Right to Object	Within one month	In any form e.g. email or orally	Search for data relating to the request e.g. the marketing data.	Consider whether objection is appropriate. Stop processing the data if request is meritorious. Consider Article 21 GDPR.	No.

7. **The Right to have human oversight in a decision made by a computer**	Within one month	In any form e.g. email or orally	Consider whether a computer did make the decision without human involvement that significantly affected the person.	Ensure human intervention in the decision, if appropriate. Consider Article 22 GDPR.	No.

Practical Steps to take:

1. **Policy** – Put a Data Subject Rights Policy and Procedure in place so staff are aware of the company obligations for complying with all GDPR Data Subject Requests from customers or employees. Make sure someone within the company is responsible for processing and responding to any GDPR Rights Requests.
2. **Training** – Ensure relevant employees are trained on how to recognise and respond to Data Subject Rights, including front line staff.
3. **Searching** – Ensure your company is able to search across the organisation for data relating to the Data Subject Request, such as an Access or Erasure Request. Check with your IT Department to make sure they can find, access and delete the personal data of any customer or employee on request.
4. **Software** – Consider purchasing software tools to allow your company to automate the Data Subjects Rights processes, including tools to locate data, redact data and provide data.

CHAPTER FOURTEEN
MERGERS AND ACQUISITIONS AND GDPR

Mergers and Acquisitions

Financial Services is a very fast-moving sector. Companies in this sector are often involved in Mergers and Acquisitions ('M&A').

This short chapter looks briefly at some of the GDPR issues that relate to Mergers and Acquisitions.

What is a Merger?

A merger is an agreement that unites two existing companies into one new company. Mergers and acquisitions are commonly done to expand a company's reach, expand into new segments, or gain market share.[249]

What is an Acquisition?

An acquisition is when one company purchases most or all of another company's shares to gain control of that company. Acquisitions, which are very common in business, may occur with the target company's approval, or in spite of its disapproval.[250]

---

[249] Investopedia.com

[250] Investopedia.com

M&A – The £18.4 million risk

In October 2020, the ICO fined a hotel company ('Company A') £18.4 million for failing to keep millions of customers' personal data secure. This fine related to an acquisition.

A cyber-attack in 2014 was perpetrated against Company B. The attack remained undetected for 4 years until September 2018.

In the intervening period, between the attack and detection, Company B was acquired by Company A.

Company A was therefore the Controller at the time of the breach and was fined £18.4 million by the ICO.[251]

Reducing the risks on M&A Transactions

M&A and complying with the Data Protection Principles

Let's use the Data Protection Principles [252]as a guide to reducing compliance risk in relation to M&A transactions. There are many aspects to complying with the Data Protection Principles, but we outline one example of how the principles may be relevant to M&A transactions:

1. **Lawfulness, fairness and transparency**

For example, firms must ensure they have told individuals that their data may be bought or sold. Privacy Notices should reflect this. The seller should have advised the data subjects that their data may be sold to another company. The buyer should provide the data subjects with privacy information after the sale has gone through.

2. **Purpose limitation**

For example, the buyer cannot use the acquired personal data for purposes that were not originally envisaged by the seller or the data subjects, without the consent of the data subjects.

---

[251] ICO.org.uk …£18.4million for failing to keep customers' personal data secure

[252] GDPR – Article 5

3. **Data minimisation**

Firms should not process more personal data than is necessary. For example, the seller should not share more personal data than is necessary to prospective buyers before or after the sale.

4. **Accuracy**

For example, firms should take reasonable steps to ensure the data they retain on customers is accurate before the sale goes through. Buyers should take care to ascertain that the data they obtain is accurate.

5. **Storage limitation**

For example, old or obsolete data should be deleted before the sale goes through if appropriate to do so, to comply with the Storage Limitation Principle.

6. **Security**

As part of the Due Diligence process, buyers must ensure that appropriate security is in place by the seller because as soon as the target is acquired, the buyer will be responsible for the personal data security and liable for any personal data breaches that occur.

7. **Accountability**

For example, buyers should keep records of the Due Diligence conducted on the seller's privacy controls pre-sale.

Due Diligence

During the Due Diligence Process, the buyer should assess the seller to see the extent of the data protection risk posed by acquiring the seller.

If the seller's house is not in order, then this poses a risk to the buyer because the buyer will be the Controller after the sale goes through and will be responsible for any data protection breaches or GDPR infringements. This can be expensive as highlighted by the £18.4 million fine above (See **M&A – The £18.4 million risk**).

How should the buyer conduct Due Diligence on the seller?

The prospective buyer should assess the seller's data protection compliance. The buyer should send the seller a written questionnaire during negotiations, asking them to set out:

- **Data** – The type of personal data being acquired.
- **Security** – The security controls in place in relation to the data.
- **Fines** – Whether the seller has faced any sanctions from Data Protection Authorities.
- **Complaints** -The number of complaints the seller has received from customers on personal data issues.
- **Privacy Program** – Evidence of the seller's Privacy Program, including asking to see the Seller's Privacy Notices, Policies, DPIAs and Security Controls.

If there are gaps in the Seller's compliance, then this will help the buyer understand the risk profile of acquiring the target.

Due Diligence- Don't share more than is necessary.

During the Due Diligence Process, personal data should only be shared where this is absolutely necessary. Sharing more data than this poses risks for the seller and the buyer.

If the buyer shares data unnecessarily during negotiations, then this could pose a security risk for the buyer.

Equally, if the buyer accepts data unnecessarily during negotiations, then the buyer will be responsible for keeping that personal data securely and could be liable for it if it is lost or compromised.

During negotiations, it is unlikely that the buyer will need to see too much of the seller's personal data. The seller should anonymise personal data if they can, to reduce the risk in this area.

Data Protection Impact Assessment

The prospective buyer should perform a DPIA at the beginning of negotiations. This will help the buyer to mitigate any data protection risks in relation to the purchase. The DPIA should document the risk mitigations in place including:

- Working with the seller to ensure personal data is not shared unnecessarily.
- Putting security controls in place such as encryption or anonymisation when data is shared.
- Ensuring an appropriate transfer mechanism is in place if data is to be transferred internationally.

The seller should also conduct its own DPIA before the sale to make sure any privacy risks on its side are mitigated.

See Chapter 3 for more details on DPIAs.

International Transfers

The buyer and seller should ensure there are appropriate transfer mechanisms in place to allow international transfers of personal data to take place. Standard Contractual Clauses are the most likely transfer mechanism between the seller and buyer if personal data is being transferred to a third country.

See Chapter 2 for more details on Transfers.

Security

Security is perhaps the riskiest part of M&A transactions. Vast swathes of data can be moved from the seller to the buyer during negotiations and especially after the sale goes through.

The sheer amount of personal data being transferred can represent data on millions of customers accumulated by the seller over many decades.

The seller is expected to have security in place appropriate to the risk.[253]

In other words, the seller must ensure that appropriate security is in place at all times, both before and after the sale. The security may include encryption, anonymisation, staff training and other measures.

The buyer also needs to be careful in relation to Security.

The buyer will be the Controller after the sale goes through (See para above M&A – **The £18.4 million risk**). At that point, they will be responsible for all of the data protection compliance. The buyer should ensure that they identify any security gaps in the newly-acquired data so they can put controls in place to remediate those gaps after the sale.

The Sale Contract

The buyer should put a contract in place. The contract should contain indemnities from the seller that their data protection compliance has been accurately described to the buyer. In the event that anything adverse does happen post-sale, such as a data breach that is the fault of the seller, the buyer can potentially seek damages from the seller.

You bought it, you own it...

After the buyer has acquired the target, a full Audit of Data Protection Compliance at the newly-acquired business should take place.

Questionnaires should be sent to all central functions and parts of the newly acquired business.

Gaps should be recorded, and remediation work should take place to bring the newly-acquired business into compliance.

---

[253] GDPR – Article 32

Recap and practical steps to take:

1. **Security** – The seller should not share more personal data than is necessary before or after the sale. The buyer should not accept more data than is necessary from the seller before or after the sale. Both sides of the transaction should ensure there are adequate security controls in place around any data that is shared before or after the sale.

2. **Data Protection Impact Assessment** – A DPIA should be completed by the buyer before any M&A transaction goes through. The seller should also consider doing a DPIA to mitigate its own risks. See Chapter 3 for more details on DPIAs. This will help mitigate the risks relating to the M&A transaction.

3. **Due Diligence** – The buyer should conduct Due Diligence on the Seller's Privacy Program before purchase. The buyer will be responsible for any data that it acquires from the seller. The buyer should therefore make sure there is adequate Due Diligence performed on the data.

4. **Contracts** – The buyer should put a contract in place with the seller with indemnities in place in case anything does go wrong with data protection compliance after the sale that is not the fault of the new buyer.

5. **Transfers** – If data is being sent internationally, then there should be an appropriate transfer mechanism in place that facilitates the sale.

MORE BOOKS BY LAW BRIEF PUBLISHING

A selection of our other titles available now:-

'A Practical Guide to Solicitor and Client Costs – 2nd Edition' by Robin Dunne
'Constructive Dismissal – Practice Pointers and Principles' by Benjimin Burgher
'A Practical Guide to Religion and Belief Discrimination Claims in the Workplace' by Kashif Ali
'A Practical Guide to the Law of Medical Treatment Decisions' by Ben Troke
'Fundamental Dishonesty and QOCS in Personal Injury Proceedings: Law and Practice' by Jake Rowley
'A Practical Guide to the Law in Relation to School Exclusions' by Charlotte Hadfield & Alice de Coverley
'A Practical Guide to Divorce for the Silver Separators' by Karin Walker
'The Right to be Forgotten – The Law and Practical Issues' by Melissa Stock
'A Practical Guide to Planning Law and Rights of Way in National Parks, the Broads and AONBs' by James Maurici QC, James Neill et al
'A Practical Guide to Election Law' by Tom Tabori
'A Practical Guide to the Law in Relation to Surrogacy' by Andrew Powell
'A Practical Guide to Claims Arising from Fatal Accidents – 2nd Edition' by James Patience
'A Practical Guide to the Ownership of Employee Inventions – From Entitlement to Compensation' by James Tumbridge & Ashley Roughton
'A Practical Guide to Asbestos Claims' by Jonathan Owen & Gareth McAloon
'A Practical Guide to Stamp Duty Land Tax in England and Northern Ireland' by Suzanne O'Hara
'A Practical Guide to the Law of Farming Partnerships' by Philip Whitcomb

'Covid-19, Homeworking and the Law – The Essential Guide to Employment and GDPR Issues' by Forbes Solicitors
'Covid-19, Force Majeure and Frustration of Contracts – The Essential Guide' by Keith Markham
'Covid-19 and Criminal Law – The Essential Guide' by Ramya Nagesh
'Covid-19 and Family Law in England and Wales – The Essential Guide' by Safda Mahmood
'A Practical Guide to the Law of Unlawful Eviction and Harassment – 2nd Edition' by Stephanie Lovegrove
'Covid-19, Residential Property, Equity Release and Enfranchisement – The Essential Guide' by Paul Sams and Louise Uphill
'Covid-19, Brexit and the Law of Commercial Leases – The Essential Guide' by Mark Shelton
'A Practical Guide to Costs in Personal Injury Claims – 2nd Edition' by Matthew Hoe
'A Practical Guide to the General Data Protection Regulation (GDPR) – 2nd Edition' by Keith Markham
'Ellis on Credit Hire – Sixth Edition' by Aidan Ellis & Tim Kevan
'A Practical Guide to Working with Litigants in Person and McKenzie Friends in Family Cases' by Stuart Barlow
'Protecting Unregistered Brands: A Practical Guide to the Law of Passing Off' by Lorna Brazell
'A Practical Guide to Secondary Liability and Joint Enterprise Post-Jogee' by Joanne Cecil & James Mehigan
'A Practical Guide to the Pre-Action RTA Claims Protocol for Personal Injury Lawyers' by Antonia Ford
'A Practical Guide to Neighbour Disputes and the Law' by Alexander Walsh
'A Practical Guide to Forfeiture of Leases' by Mark Shelton
'A Practical Guide to Coercive Control for Legal Practitioners and Victims' by Rachel Horman

'A Practical Guide to Rights Over Airspace and Subsoil' by Daniel Gatty
'Tackling Disclosure in the Criminal Courts – A Practitioner's Guide' by Narita Bahra QC & Don Ramble
'A Practical Guide to the Law of Driverless Cars – Second Edition' by Alex Glassbrook, Emma Northey & Scarlett Milligan
'A Practical Guide to TOLATA Claims' by Greg Williams
'Artificial Intelligence – The Practical Legal Issues' by John Buyers
'A Practical Guide to the Law of Prescription in Scotland' by Andrew Foyle
'A Practical Guide to the Construction and Rectification of Wills and Trust Instruments' by Edward Hewitt
'A Practical Guide to the Law of Bullying and Harassment in the Workplace' by Philip Hyland
'How to Be a Freelance Solicitor: A Practical Guide to the SRA-Regulated Freelance Solicitor Model' by Paul Bennett
'A Practical Guide to Prison Injury Claims' by Malcolm Johnson
'A Practical Guide to the Small Claims Track' by Dominic Bright
'A Practical Guide to Advising Clients at the Police Station' by Colin Stephen McKeown-Beaumont
'A Practical Guide to Antisocial Behaviour Injunctions' by Iain Wightwick
'Practical Mediation: A Guide for Mediators, Advocates, Advisers, Lawyers, and Students in Civil, Commercial, Business, Property, Workplace, and Employment Cases' by Jonathan Dingle with John Sephton
'The Mini-Pupillage Workbook' by David Boyle
'A Practical Guide to Crofting Law' by Brian Inkster
'A Practical Guide to Spousal Maintenance' by Liz Cowell
'A Practical Guide to the Law of Domain Names and Cybersquatting' by Andrew Clemson
'A Practical Guide to the Law of Gender Pay Gap Reporting' by Harini Iyengar

'A Practical Guide to the Rights of Grandparents in Children Proceedings' by Stuart Barlow
'NHS Whistleblowing and the Law' by Joseph England
'Employment Law and the Gig Economy' by Nigel Mackay & Annie Powell
'A Practical Guide to Noise Induced Hearing Loss (NIHL) Claims' by Andrew Mckie, Ian Skeate, Gareth McAloon
'An Introduction to Beauty Negligence Claims – A Practical Guide for the Personal Injury Practitioner' by Greg Almond
'Intercompany Agreements for Transfer Pricing Compliance' by Paul Sutton
'Zen and the Art of Mediation' by Martin Plowman
'A Practical Guide to the SRA Principles, Individual and Law Firm Codes of Conduct 2019 – What Every Law Firm Needs to Know' by Paul Bennett
'A Practical Guide to Adoption for Family Lawyers' by Graham Pegg
'A Practical Guide to Industrial Disease Claims' by Andrew Mckie & Ian Skeate
'A Practical Guide to Redundancy' by Philip Hyland
'A Practical Guide to Vicarious Liability' by Mariel Irvine
'A Practical Guide to Applications for Landlord's Consent and Variation of Leases' by Mark Shelton
'A Practical Guide to Relief from Sanctions Post-Mitchell and Denton' by Peter Causton
'A Practical Guide to Equity Release for Advisors' by Paul Sams
'A Practical Guide to the Law Relating to Food' by Ian Thomas
'A Practical Guide to Financial Services Claims' by Chris Hegarty
'The Law of Houses in Multiple Occupation: A Practical Guide to HMO Proceedings' by Julian Hunt
'A Practical Guide to Unlawful Eviction and Harassment' by Stephanie Lovegrove
'Occupiers, Highways and Defective Premises Claims: A Practical Guide Post-Jackson – 2nd Edition' by Andrew Mckie

www.ingramcontent.com/pod-product-compliance
Lightning Source LLC
LaVergne TN
LVHW052323200926
848481LV00002B/652
9781913715830